The Reinhold Book of Art Ideas

Top row, left: Portrait of a Woman by John Sargent, pencil. (Reproduced by permission of the Metropolitan Museum of Fine Art, gift of Mrs. Francis Ormond, 1950.) *Center: Face and Hands* (detail) by Fernand Léger, ink. (Reproduced by permission of the Museum of Modern Art, New York, Mrs. Wendell T. Bush Fund.) *Right: Portrait of a Girl* (detail) by Diego Velasquez, chalk. (Courtesy of the British Museum.)

Center row, left: Detail of sketch by Norman Laliberté, oil crayon and pencil. *Center: No. 6-1965* (detail) by Richard Lindner, collage. (Reproduced courtesy of Cordier & Ekstrom, Inc., New York.) *Right: The Death Chamber* (detail) by Edvard Munch, silhouette. (Reproduced by permission of the Museum of Modern Art, New York.)

Bottom row, left: Detail from an 18th-century deck of tarot cards, woodcut. *Center:* Detail from a vase depicting Mycenaean warriors marching to battle, stencil. (Reproduced courtesy of the National Museum, Athens.) *Right:* Detail from a bronze head, court of Benin, Africa, 16th to 17th century. (Reproduced by permission of the Museum of Primitive Art, New York.)

The Reinhold Book of Art Ideas

History and Techniques

Norman Laliberté/Alex Mogelon

Van Nostrand Reinhold Company
New York Cincinnati London Toronto Melbourne

To Sterling McIlhany

Van Nostrand Reinhold Company Regional Offices:
New York Cincinnati Chicago Millbrae Dallas
Van Nostrand Reinhold Company International Offices:
London Toronto Melbourne

Published by Van Nostrand Reinhold Company
A Division of Litton Educational Publishing, Inc.
450 West 33rd Street, New York, N.Y. 10001

16 15 14 13 12 11 10 9 8 7 6 5 4 3 2 1

Library of Congress Cataloging in Publication Data

Laliberté, Norman.
    Reinhold book of art ideas.

    SUMMARY: Demonstrates uses of nine media, including woodcuts, collage,
and ink, with a discussion of the history and development of each.
    1. Art—Handbooks, manuals, etc.—Juvenile literature. [1. Art—Technique]
I. Mogelon, Alex, joint author. II. Title. III. Title. Book of art ideas.
N7440.L34   702'.8   75-5150
ISBN 0-442-24611-0

The authors and Van Nostrand Reinhold Company have taken all possible care to
trace the ownership of every work of art reproduced in this book and to make full
acknowledgment for its use. If any errors have accidentally occurred, they will be
corrected in subsequent editions, provided notification is sent to the publisher.

Also by the authors:
Art in Boxes (1974)
The Art of Monoprint (1974)

Selections in the present volume have been excerpted by arrangement with Art
Horizons, Inc. from the following books by the authors:
Drawing with Pencils (1969)
Drawing with Ink (1970)
Pastel, Charcoal and Chalk Drawing (1973)
Painting with Crayons (1967)
Collage, Montage, Assemblage (1971)
Silhouettes, Shadows and Cutouts (1968)
Twentieth Century Woodcuts (1971)
The Art of Stencil (1971)
Masks, Face Coverings and Headgear (1973)

Details on front cover by Norman Laliberté, *from
left to right:* (1) colored pencil drawing; (2) collage;
(3) *Flowering Madonna,* collage with decals; (4) oil
crayon drawing with stencilled numbers.

Details on back cover by Norman Laliberté, *from
left to right:* (1) collage; (2) collage with felt-tipped
pen and watercolor; (3) pastel; (4) collage.

Contents

Introduction

This compendium of art ideas, demonstrations, and projects contains selections from nine of our previous books, which we feel will be most useful in secondary school classrooms, although many of the illustrations and suggestions can be adapted for use on other levels of art education. For example, the section by Beatrice Thompson, in the chapter on pastel, charcoal, and chalk drawing, contains techniques a teacher may present to advanced pupils to create rich, professional works of art.

Of particular interest to the teacher who does not have a large art library near at hand is the art history section in each one of the chapters. It includes history and development of the medium being discussed, and its use by old masters, modern masters, and contemporary artists. Each chapter then goes on to give project suggestions, many of them in finished examples done by Norman Laliberté over the years, and step-by-step demonstrations.

The presentation of each medium is designed to stimulate interest in its traditional use while encouraging students to experiment and develop individual techniques. The section on drawing with pencil stresses that the medium is a fully developed means to

artistic expression, with illustrations from Goya, Hogarth, Picasso, Saul Steinberg, and others. The section on drawing with ink shows how bold and contemporary this many-centuries-old medium can appear to the modern eye, as Dürer, Matisse, and Baskin help to illustrate.

Few contemporary artists and teachers are familiar with the flexible and beautiful results produced by pastel, charcoal, and chalk media. In the past they have been used mostly for preliminary studies, but in the hands of the skillful a wide variety of effects can be obtained that are usually associated only with oil and synthetic media. Oil crayons and wax crayons are explored in the chapter on painting with crayons, which presents master crayon drawings of the 19th and 20th centuries, such as those of Kokoschka, Kollwitz, Degas, and Klee, as well as a glimpse at the early wax technique of encaustic.

Several chapters stress the graphic use that can be made of cut paper forms, outlines, and the shapes of things themselves, as for example in collage, montage, and assemblage or silhouettes, shadows, and cutouts or the various artistic uses of stencils. There are suggestions for how to acquire materials, combine them in effective patterns, and vary

the piece with personal statements in painting and drawing techniques. There is a demonstration of combined collage and printmaking, interesting views of Polish paper-cutting and Oriental shadow theater, as well as contemporary illustrations of the use of stencils in the work of Pop Artists such as Johns, Warhol, and Indiana.

The chapter on woodcuts demonstrates printmaking with principles that can be applied to several other graphic techniques, and students will discover an exciting new means to express personal images through the techniques illustrated and explored in the section on masks, face coverings, and headgear. The results of work in paper, cloth, and cardboard are many times whimsical and playful, which can help stimulate imagination and expressiveness. The use of art techniques on textiles can serve as an introduction to the growing interest in art fabrics and soft sculpture.

Here, then, is *The Reinhold Book of Art Ideas*. We hope it will serve as still another tool in creating additional interest in the nine media explored, and as a catalyst to experimentation by the student toward development of unique artistic expression.

Young Hare. Pencil drawing by Goya, after the famous watercolor by Dürer, executed in 1502. Pencil was often used by the masters to copy the work of predecessors as an exercise in technique and facility. In his original watercolor, Dürer precisely defined each hair of the animal. Goya's eighteenth-century pencil copy gives the fur a soft, almost silken texture. (Courtesy Fernand Hazen Editions, Paris; Methuen and Co., Ltd., London; and Tudor Publishing Company, New York, publishers of *Look, or the Keys of Art,* by John Canaday, Photograph by Paul David.)

DRAWING WITH PENCIL

Early Pencil Drawing

Drawing is considered by many to be the earliest art technique known to man. Its most ancient forms are found in the cave pictures of the Stone Age, in rock inscriptions and scratchings executed by nomadic peoples in many parts of the world, and in the art of the early inhabitants of the Orient, whose brush drawings, in time, developed into a form of calligraphy.

Early drawings may have been created for religious, ritual or magical purposes, if not for reasons of basic communication or pure artistic expression. With the advent of economical methods for the manufacture of paper in the fifteenth century, it became a basic procedure for most artists and architects in the Western world to execute a multitude of preliminary drawings and sketches to delineate composition, to define detail, and to plan size and scale prior to commencing a major work.

As a drawing instrument, the pencil is a recent medium, having been preceded in concept and use by varieties of ink, chalk, charcoal, paint, and the silver point. This latter device (and, similarly, the instrument known as the metal point) developed from the ancient stylus. It incorporated a point of copper, lead or other minerals and was drawn over paper coated with an abrasive surface of lead white and a glue or gum binding solution, which caught and held fine particles of the metal, thus forming a line. The line would later darken and dull to assume a warm tonal quality.

The everyday graphite pencil ("lead" is a misnomer) developed following the delicate, precise, linear effects achieved through the silver point and metal point in master drawings by Dürer, Leonardo da Vinci, and Raphael. Graphite was discovered in England and put to use in various types of holders by artists and draftsmen in the sixteenth century. By the seventeenth century, because of its facility, graphite competed with ink, chalk, and other media in the execution of drawings preliminary to major works; Dutch and Flemish masters added small areas of graphite drawing to depict sharp details in some of their major works painted in oils.

In the eighteenth century, the French scientist and inventor, Conté, encouraged by Napoleon, developed the prototype of the pencil as we know it today. Though graphite had been encased in wood previous to this, in 1795 Conté mixed the impure French graphite (finely ground to a powder) with clay and kiln-baked it to a hard and firm substance which is commonly referred to as "lead." Within a short space of time, this manufacturing process was improved upon in Germany and England. Before long, artists were drawing with graphite pencil and discovering the wide range of effects it made possible, including shade and tone qualities brought about by rubbing and delicate light and heavy hard-line characteristics. An additional attribute was that the graphite pencil could be used on the surface of almost any substance.

Among the masters who used the graphite pencil were Gainsborough and Romney, who, in the eighteenth century, presented finished works in this medium; the French artist Ingres, whose lucid and elegant pencil portraits are to be found in many of the world's museums; Edgar Degas, who worked with soft, medium, and hard pencils to explore a full range of potentialities in one composition; Delacroix, who found the graphite pencil a ready ally in his wish to conceive and complete a composition speedily; and the sculptor Rodin, who experimented with pencil in elements of space and scale in the planning of his masterpieces.

To this day, the graphite pencil continues to be an efficient and effective tool for the execution of sketches and concepts that are preliminary to finished work in other media. But in an era when speed of execution and the impact of initial impressions are steadfastly making headway within the scale of standards of the visual arts, the pencil is a fully recognized medium of artistic expression, an instrument of the vitality and intense spirit of the time in which it has come into its own.

Le Nouveau Né. Pencil drawing by Jean François Millet (1814-1875). Many of Millet's subjects depicted working people, and he was often accused of being a socialist. His wish ''to make the trivial serve to express the sublime'' may have been aided by the pencil, with which he sketched details of composition preliminary to completing works in both pastels and oils. (Reproduced by permission of the National Gallery of Art, Rosenwald Collection, Washington, D.C.)

Artists and draftsmen of the nineteenth century worked hand in hand with archaeologists in recording — by means of pencil drawings — intricate details and initial impressions of explorations in the tombs of the pharaohs. These drawings by E. W. Lane and J. Bonomi were made in 1826-27 and depict the cornice and vault of the Temple of Sethos I, a view of the façade and interior of the cliff temple of Abu Simbel, and the pyramid of Chephren. (Photographs courtesy British Museum, London.)

Simon and Garfunkel.
Pencil drawings by Saul
Lambert for Columbia
Records. A unique feature
of the graphite pencil is
its ability to delineate
detail with a soft tonal
quality. (Courtesy
Columbia Broadcasting
System.)

Detail of *War Games* by
Norman Laliberté.

Contemporary Pencil Drawings

The word "pencil" is derived from the Latin *penicillum*, meaning a little tail, which refers to the very fine brushes used for writing during the period in which the word was conceived.

Though the first pencil-manufacturing business was opened by Kaspar Faber in Germany in 1761 (using a composition of graphite and sulphur), it was not until 1812, when war halted European imports, that graphite pencils were manufactured in the United States, by William Monroe, a Massachusetts hardware dealer. In 1827, Joseph Dixon began manufacturing pencils in Salem, Massachusetts, in what was the beginning of the multi-million-dollar industry conducted by some 15 manufacturers in the United States today. By 1876, pencil graphite had changed from square to round in shape and, in time, colored pencils and graphite of more durable and varying qualities were developed.

For the contemporary artist, drawing with pencil helps meet the challenge of capturing the immediate. Just as the reporter at the scene of an event quickly records in a notebook facts and background to be elaborated upon once he returns to his typewriter, so, in many instances, does the artist sketch and delineate detail with pencil preliminary to work on a fuller scale in other media.

Drawing has been termed by many the closest contact the artist can have with creativity. In an age when speed is a major element of life, the artist frequently finds that drawing simply must convey more than strokes and symbols that give the illusion of three-dimensional form. In many instances it must have a function greater than being simply an intermediary step to a major work in oils, watercolor or gouache. If the reporter's notes were to be printed word for word, they would lack the embellishment and background detail that the finished news story possesses. But they would surely convey more of the dynamism and impact of the precise moment in which they were written. This, in essence, is what many contemporary artists seek to capture by drawing a scene, a vignette or an event for drawing's sake alone.

The facility, efficiency, and many effective graphic qualities of the graphite pencil enable the artist to record both impact and mood. Though every artist learns technique from predecessors and contemporaries, the time he lives in and the experiences he endures remain his greatest teachers. Many pencil drawings of this century convey more than a recognizable technique or picture. They capture and preserve an idea with immediacy and force.

The historian, by word, phrase, and fact, records the story of a nation. The artist, by drawing, records visually the journey of a people through time. Drawing is spontaneity, feeling, and mood—the agility of a child walking on a fence, the tension of a street demonstration. Drawing captures the tenderness between lovers, the impact of hockey players colliding, the fright on the face of a young man at war.

By drawing, the artist records the social values and the social changes of his generation and the tastes, patterns, and happenings of the everyday life that is his environment. Many of these, like time itself, are fleeting. Like the writer and the photographer, the pencil artist is emerging as an historian of our era.

Pencil drawing by Saul Steinberg. Steinberg, whom many consider to be the greatest master of satire in America, draws with great freedom. His sense of control and discipline enable him to project his thinking in a seemingly continuous line, with a minimum of detail. (Courtesy Hallmark, Kansas City, Missouri.)

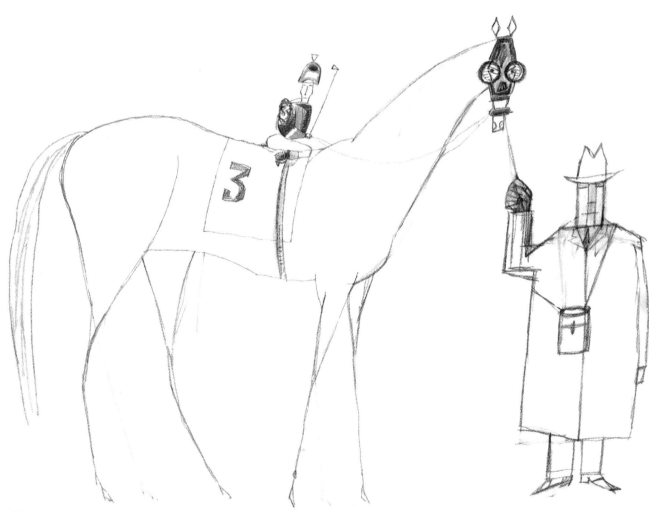

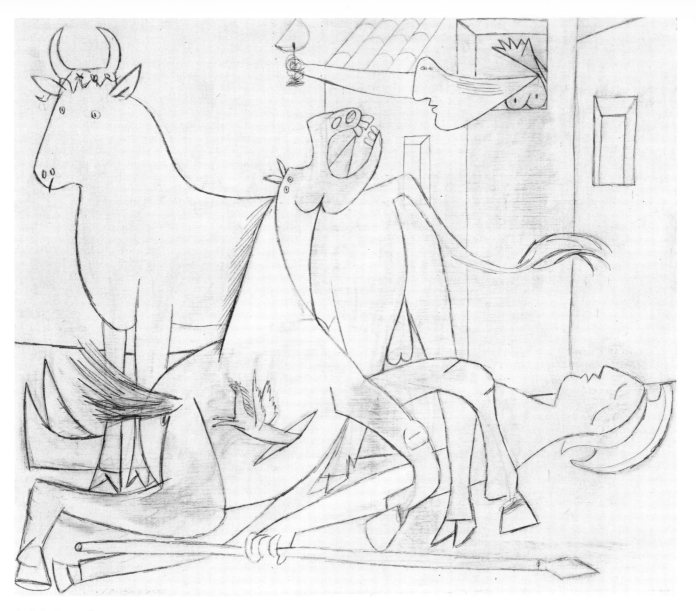

Study for Guernica by
Pablo Picasso, 1937. Pencil
on gesso on wool. Pre-
liminary drawing for one
of the artist's major
works during the Spanish
Civil War, symbolizing
man's inhumanity to man.
(Reproduced courtesy of
the Museum of Modern
Art, New York, gift of the
artist. Photo by Malcolm
Varon.)

15

Family Portrait. Pencil study by
Larry Rivers. (Courtesy The Museum
of Modern Art, New York.)

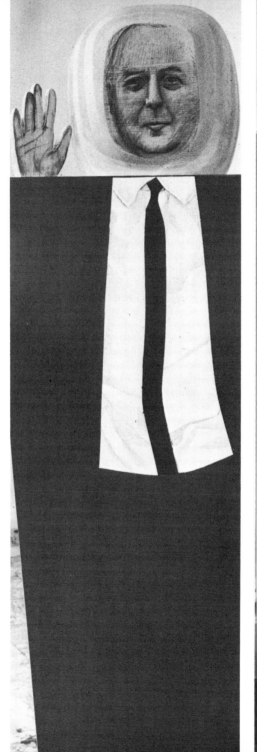

The Heads of State.
Sculptures by Marisol
showing examples of
pencil drawing on paper
and wood to depict facial
form and personality
characteristics.

Left. Mao Tse Tung. The
face is composed of pencil
over paper sculpture.
(Collection of Conrad
Janis, New York. Photo
by Geoffrey Clements.)

Center. The Rt. Hon.
Harold Wilson. Pencil
and mixed media on wood
form the face. (Collection
of Evan M. Frankel,
Easthampton, Long
Island. Photo by J. S.
Lewinski, F.R.P.S.)

Right. Generalisimo
Francisco Franco. The
head is composed of
pencil and mixed media on
paper. (Collection of
Evan M. Frankel,
Easthampton, Long
Island. Photo by Geoffrey
Clements. Courtesy
Sidney Janis Gallery,
New York.)

The ever-jostling throng of irrepressible Britain. Pencil drawing of Piccadilly by Paul Hogarth. Like the newsreporter with a microphone, the artist has caught the exciting confusion of a city on the move in an on-the-spot pencil drawing. (From *London A La Mode*, by Malcolm Muggeridge and Paul Hogarth, published by Hill and Wang, Inc., New York.)

The Judges. Pencil composition by David Aronson. Pencil strokes and shadings depict the weight and melancholy of decision. (Collection of the Whitney Museum of American Art, New York. Gift of Mr. and Mrs. Chauncey Waddell. Photo by Geoffrey Clements.)

Above. The Spanish Guitar Player.

Left. Famille Valaranne. 1952.
Pencil studies by René Auberjonois.
Auberjonois' drawings possess
strength and stature and, at the same
time, an aura of mystery. Though
many of his pencil drawings were
preliminary to major paintings, his
delicate, determined lines were said
to be closer to the true nature of the
subject than the final work, which
may have lost vitality and intensity
in the technique of brushstroke and in
color. By means of pencil drawing,
Auberjonois conveyed what *Graphis*
described as ". . . the uniqueness of
life, which he comprehends in the act
of drawing it." (Reproduced by
arrangement with S.P.A.D.E.M.,
Paris. Photographs courtesy Walter
Herdeg, *Graphis*, Zurich.)

The American Way: Eat #3 by Robert Indiana. Conté rubbing. (Courtesy Stable Gallery, New York. Photo by John D. Schiff.)

22

Detail of *War Games* by
Norman Laliberté.

Pencil Demonstration with Multimedia Techniques

There is an amazing range of pencil media and technical effects at the fingertips of the contemporary student and professional draftsman. The visual demonstration in this chapter was created by Norman Laliberté, and represents a tableau of musicians done in the tradition of decorative Medieval and Renaissance court painting. In it the artist uses an extraordinary variety of drawing media and techniques, beginning with soft and hard graphite pencils and finishing with colored pencils, washes, inks, dyes, oil crayon accents, and collage.

As the demonstration unfolds step by step, the viewer can follow the evolution of the drawings at close range and in detail. Unlike many such demonstrations, it is not intended to acquaint the student with new subject matter, but to reveal how, in the hands of an imaginative draftsman, media, techniques, and style join to produce a work of art.

(The demonstration photographs are by Fortune Monte.)

Opposite Page

A project for continuing a photograph uses portions of pasted-down photographic material that are completed or extended with the addition of gray and black pencil details.

Musicians by Norman Laliberté

1. Some of the pencils used in the demonstration, including soft, medium, and hard graphite pencils and a wide range of color pencils.

2. The beginning of a preliminary, multi-media drawing. With a medium graphite pencil, the general theme or basic concept is sketched out in quick outline in order to establish the boundaries of the drawing. Color pencils are employed to establish and further block in some areas of the drawing.

3. Bits and pieces of graphic materials are added. Color sections of different shapes and sizes are cut from a printed party card. These cut-out elements can be of various weights and textures of paper, from light tissue to heavy cardboard. They build up the surface and give the drawing an added dimension.

4. The cut-out portion is placed on the drawing to accentuate the pencil detail, and glued down.

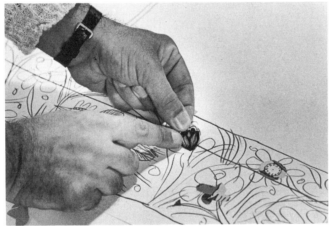

5. More cut-outs, large and small, are pasted down. The cut-outs need not be related to the drawing but may serve, as in this case, to augment the texture of the composition.

6. More details are added to the lower section of the drawing with regular graphite pencil.

7. The details are refined with color pencils.

8. Pencil detail, more positive in character, is added. Then, colored inks are applied with a brush to fill in open areas. A thin brush is used for fine details, a thicker one to apply wash overlays.

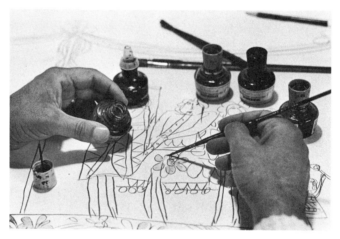

9. Dr. Martin's dyes are used to fill in other areas of the drawing. These dyes lend richness of tone and brilliant color.

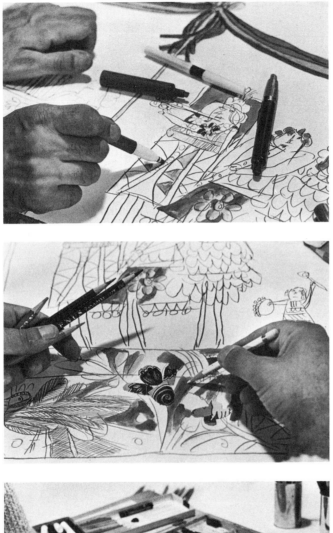

10. Some penciled areas, as well as sections painted with ink and dye, are covered with designs made with felt-nib pens of various colors. The pen lines strengthen the drawing, defining some areas and giving a general glazing effect. Light, medium or heavy textures can be achieved by varying the pressure.

11. A white pencil is used to re-draw over the ink. This clarifies elements of the drawing still further and brings out finer detail in the ink areas.

12. Oil crayon is applied over pencil, washes, and cut-out portions of the drawing to achieve uniformity of texture in certain areas.

13. Oil crayon is again dragged over the drawing. When pressure is applied to the crayon, the graphite pencil lines smear and blur, creating the impression of movement.

14. Oil crayon and dye surfaces are scratched with various sharp tools including an X-acto knife. Different tools, such as razor blades, nails, and pins, make scratched-in lines with manifold characteristics.

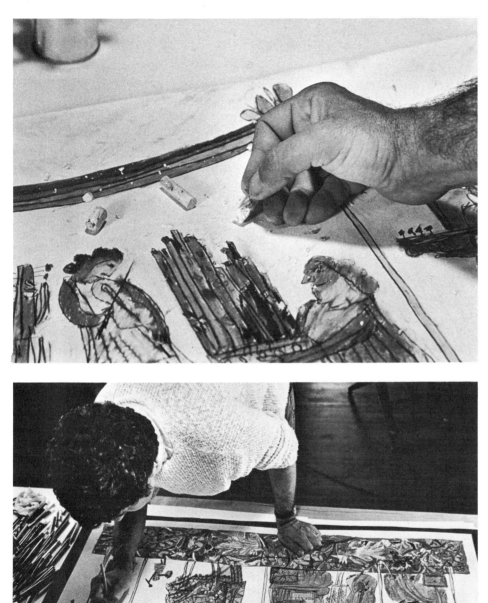

15. Minute amounts of colored crayon are deposited here and there in the bare sections of the drawing. A white oil crayon is then applied over all of the bare sections and the particles of color are dissolved and smeared into the white. This completely eliminates the flat effect of a bare paper background and gives body, texture, and a finished appearance to the work.

16. Final touches are achieved with graphite and color pencils.

17. *The Musicians* is completed.

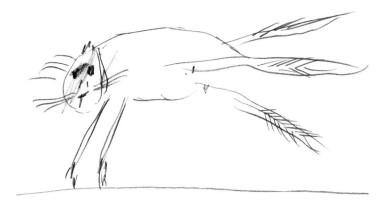

Pencil drawing of a cat
by Norman Laliberté.

Pencil Projects

The pencil lends itself to a number of projects which bring its facility for speed and spontaneity into play. These include tracing, rubbing, and shading, the extension of printed photographs or illustrations clipped from a magazine or newspaper, the embellishment with graphite and color pencils of cutouts and ripouts, pencil drawings built around calligraphy and typography, and the use of various pencil techniques to achieve hard or soft textures, grays or shadow effects.

This chapter illustrates some of these projects, many of which are employed in schoolrooms across the country and by students exploring the wide range of techniques that the graphite and color pencil are capable of achieving.

Page 32. Transfer. The outline of an illustration from a magazine is transferred by means of a sheet of carbon onto a piece of paper. Then a second illustration of a different figure (from another magazine page) is transferred in the same way onto the same sheet of paper, overlapping the first figure. The process is repeated a third time with still another illustration. The three outline illustrations, now drawn off register one on top of the other on a single sheet of paper, form an interesting design, which is colored, highlighted, and shaded with pencils.

Page 33. Silver pencil rubbing. A drawing is made on soft paper with a silver pencil. Then a graphite pencil is rubbed over the paper. The white (silver) line emerges through the rubbing. The quality of the emerging lines can be varied by controlling the application of the graphite pencil.

Page 34. Ripout. The figures are ripped out of black paper. White pencil on the black paper and black pencil around it provide detail and embellishment. The jagged, torn lines of the figures contrast with the precise pencil lines. In the example shown, a seal is added as a crowning touch.

A transfer project using magazine illustrations and carbon paper (see page 31).

Making a pencil rubbing
(see page 31).

A pencil project built around ripped-out black paper (see page 31).

34

Charlie Chaplin. Photograph extended with pencil and ink by Thomas Kelly, fourth-grade student at St. James Grammar School, Arlington, Massachusetts. The photograph, cut from a magazine or newspaper, is first pasted down. The extension of the photo is made with ink. Details are added to the outline with graphite pencil. White pencil strokes are applied on top of the ink to give further detail to the figure itself.

Mother and Child in Calèche, a white pencil drawing by Norman Laliberté. In this compressed drawing on black paper, the line is heavy and applied with even pressure throughout. The legs of the horses appear to have an x-ray, wire-like quality.

Little Girl, a soft pencil drawing by Norman Laliberté. The overall effect here is one of softness and delicacy; the drawing has an almost poetic line quality. The gray lines were achieved by rubbing with a soft graphite pencil, while the black edges emphasize the entire form. The eyes, nose, and mouth were defined with pencil to complete the figure.

Cupid and Psyche. Ink on papyrus. Made ca. 100 A.D., the drawing, discovered in Egypt, was executed (probably with a stylus made of rush) with extreme sensitivity, in the spirit of the Greek period of 550 to 300 B.C., when drawings, flat and simple in line but of monumental composition or subject matter, were used as decoration for funeral vases. (Courtesy Soprintendenza Alle Antichità, Florence, Italy.)

DRAWING WITH INK

Early History of Ink

Ink is one of the oldest writing and drawing media known to man, having originated with the Egyptian and Chinese civilizations of some 4,500 years ago. Originally, ink was compounded with lampblack, gums, and resins as the principal ingredients. The solution was dried or hardened in the form of sticks or bars. The scribe or artist dipped the end of the stick into water, then applied it to the surface which was to bear the message or drawing.

Later, extracts from plants and animals or powdered minerals were added to the ink solution to give the finished result color, tone, and a greater sense of body. The Mesopotamians were known to have dried their ink solutions in the form of oval or circular cakes or pads. The writing instrument—a reed, quill or brush—was dampened, rubbed into the solid ink solution, then applied on any of a number of surfaces including leather and linen, parchment and papyrus, vellum, pottery, clay, bone, and ivory.

Colored inks used for painting were developed in Asia—principally by the Chinese—some 1,500 years ago. The earliest Japanese art known, which dates back to 700–800 A.D., made use of ink solutions applied to cloth fabricated of hemp. Ink scroll drawings of both the Chinese and Japanese peoples of that and of successive eras have often been one of the historian's clearest insights into the life and culture of that important period in mankind's history.

As writing, drawing, and painting with ink continued, many new methods of preparing ink were developed to give it greater body, strength, and facility as a medium of communication. Charcoal was used to augment and replace lampblack. Pigments with individual characteristics were blended with basic ink solutions to produce special effects or to make possible writing or drawing on unusual surfaces. So that drawings and writing might attain a greater degree of density and qualities of permanence, particles of carbon were blended with existing ink formulas. A continuous stage of development, experimentation, discovery, and rediscovery took place as peoples of Asia and Europe, from antiquity to the Middle Ages, sought to communicate and preserve their history by writing and drawing, principally in the ink medium.

The invention of the printing press by Johann Gutenberg in the fifteenth century saw the development of many new types of inks adaptable to this revolutionary new means of communication. But scribes and artists, working mainly with inks, continued to be in demand for calligraphy and for illustration and decorative illumination of individual books, documents, and manuscripts. A number of these exist in public and private collections today and serve as eloquent testimony to the part ink has played in preserving a history of the customs, thoughts, and traditions of the period in which they were executed.

Knight On Horseback, pen and bistre with ochre brush work by Albrecht Dürer (1471-1528). There is something arresting about the knight and the dog, who appear to float in space. The static position of the horse pressed against the deep black background gives the drawing a stop-action quality. Dürer was adept at drawing and painting, woodcuts and engravings, and was a student of geometry, mathematics, languages, and literature. (Reproduced courtesy of Biblioteca Ambrosiana, Milan, Italy.)

Top row, left: Study from a fresco by Giotto (1267–1337). *Center:* Pen and ink drawing by Michelangelo (1475–1564). (Courtesy Cabinet des Dessins, Musee du Louvre, Paris.)

Right: Five Grotesque Heads, pen and ink drawing by Leonardo da Vinci (1452–1519). (Royal Library, Windsor Castle. Reproduced by gracious permission of Her Majesty Queen Elizabeth II.) Michelangelo executed myriad drawings in the process of evolving intricate detail of shape and form for his sculpture. Leonardo da Vinci did numerous drawings exploring botanical and human anatomy, though the diagram and design drawings of his inventions may be better known.

Left: Ink drawing by Peter Brueghel the Elder (1525–1569). (Reproduced with permission of the Trustees of the Pierpont Morgan Library, New York.) Peter Brueghel's drawings examined both landscapes and people with extreme sensitivity. In this immense landscape, he has given much attention to detail and has achieved fine draftsmanship by the use of the pen's full potential, so that his lines, which are not black, but gray, give the water and cloud formations a vitality of their own.

Dahlias and Pomegranates by Henri Matisse (1869-1954). Matisse, who drew this composition in 1947 with brush and ink, believed that his feelings were most directly expressed by his outline drawings. He felt that drawings with pen, brush, and ink illuminated values, expressed character, and revealed the nature of the composition's environment in the most forceful and concise manner possible. (Courtesy The Museum of Modern Art, New York, Abby Aldrich Rockefeller Purchase Fund.)

Detail from *An Essay on the Dove* by Norman Laliberté.

Master and Contemporary Ink Drawings

Ink is a vital medium of twentieth-century artistic expression. It may be applied with a brush or pen, with a cloth or sponge, with fingers or the spontaneity of dropping or dripping. What emerges is a terribly direct, strong, and uncompromising statement of the nature of our time and the talent of the artist—an individual expression of "now."

The very character of ink is challenging, demanding, and a spur to experimentation and creativity. It is a bold form of expression, sparkling clean because it is so definite and positive. Most times it defies erasure; lines or applications which the artist regrets cannot be easily concealed.

Working with ink, the artist soon develops qualities of speed, confidence, and strength. Each stroke or line is almost a rapier-thrust: there is no going back, no second chance, no stopping the line in mid-motion for an instant or two to make it longer, thicker, thinner, shorter. Every line of the drawing is for the artist a moment of truth, of pain because of limitations, of elation because of achievement.

Another challenge confronting the artist who works with ink is the accomplishment of qualities of tone. The range is limited, but the experimental possibilities are limitless. Overlapping, the relationship to each other of individual lines or areas of ink and washes, distances between shapes and forms—all of these become critical.

The drawings which appear in this section reflect the dexterity, experimentation, and innovation with which present-day artists are working in the ink medium. The student will note how ink is used to achieve texture, how a broken line is employed to convey a quality of antiquity, how the elimination of detail can many times speak more forcefully than the delineation of every feature of a subject, how line economy can accomplish excellent aspects of contrast between black and white, how the application of washes can serve to create light and dark background and foreground areas, how brush stroke applied over brush stroke succeeds in achieving qualities of volume and mass, how line qualities can be used to convey human feeling and emotion running the full gamut from depression to elation.

For the modern artist, the ink medium presents opportunities for artistic exploration and satisfaction through creativity that is extremely personal and individualistic. Because of its very nature it demands self-discipline, ingenuity, and many hours of labor and practice in which the artist can learn to master the medium by achieving results which can bring him contentment.

It has been said that ink is a medium with deep inner mysteries which the artist strives to unravel. That it can be done with full impact, beauty, and satisfaction is evidenced by the examples of ink drawing which appear herewith and by the many outstanding ink illustrations in books, periodicals, films, advertising media, graphics, and packaging to be found in every aspect of modern life.

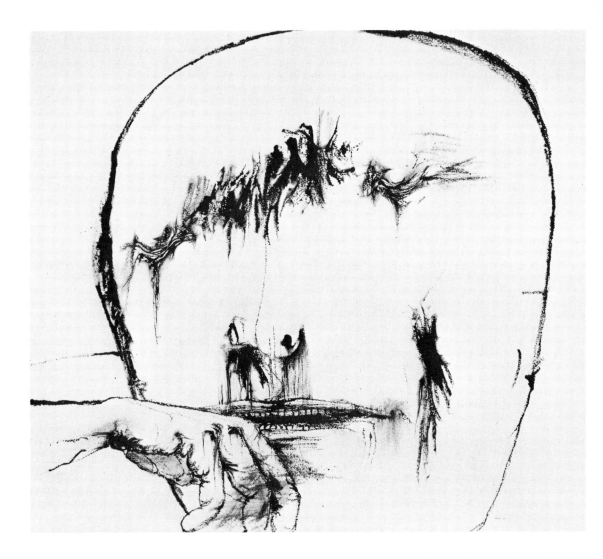

Weeping Man. Ink and pencil drawing by Leonard Baskin. The artist has positioned the subject so that it virtually floats. The overall effect conveys the feeling that the man is either falling apart or desperately striving to become something, while the line quality succeeds in evoking pathos. Superb draftsmanship allows the artist to eliminate details such as the eyes, and yet the viewer can see them. (Courtesy the Worcester Art Museum, Worcester, Mass.)

Circus drawing by
Alexander Calder from
"Imagination XI"
(courtesy of Champion
Papers). When he ex-
ecuted this drawing in
1932, Calder wrote: "I
love the space of the
circus! I made some
drawings of nothing but
the tent . . . the whole
thing of the vast space—
I've always loved it."

Madonna and Child. Pen, ink, and wash drawing by Henry Spencer Moore. In this drawing, made in preparation for a stone sculpture for the Church of St. Matthew in Northampton, the figures are set apart from the background by a water-repellent method. This was done so that the artist could visualize the mass of the forms he would eventually sculpt from stone. (Courtesy of the Cleveland Museum of Art. Hinman B. Hurlbut Collection.)

A drawing for *A Paradisiac Life* by
Klaus Warwas (Bebrauchsgraphic
International Advertising Art, Munich,
West Germany). Warwas' illustrations
have something of the quality which
compels the viewer to work at completing the picture. This drawing is
strong, massive, and appears to be
made of steel and wire rather than
with mere pen and ink. It adds a
vague suggestion of the human element
to simplified computer technology and
in its own way reduces the achieve-
ments of science to a simplified maze
of wires.

Opposite Page

Detail of ink design for gift-wrapping
paper by Bill Greer. The artist's playful
brush and pen technique employs large
black areas, very tightly defined areas,
nervous lines, and a series of dots that
serve as line. (Courtesy of Faroy, Inc.,
Houston, Texas.)

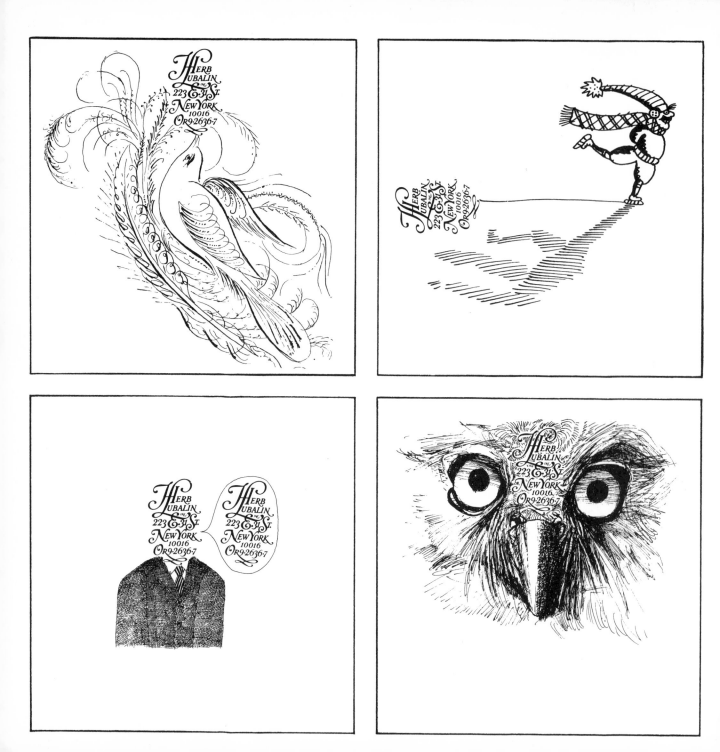

Top, left: Bird by Tony Saris. *Top, right: Skater* by Ruffins-Taback. *Bottom, left: Dinner* by Charles Slackman. *Bottom, right: Owl* by Tony Saris. (Courtesy of Herb Lubalin, Inc., New York.) The aesthetic use of pen-and-ink doodles by different artists can encompass and enhance a stylized logo or trademark. These drawings convey an impression of the personality of each artist.

Hen. Pen, brush, and india ink drawing by Saul Steinberg. The humor of the subject matter may tend to overshadow the great craftsmanship of the artist in the use of the pen. He has superb control of thick and thin lines and a marvelous sense of perspective, employing a minimal number of lines to give full impact to the landscape. (Courtesy of The Museum of Modern Art, New York.)

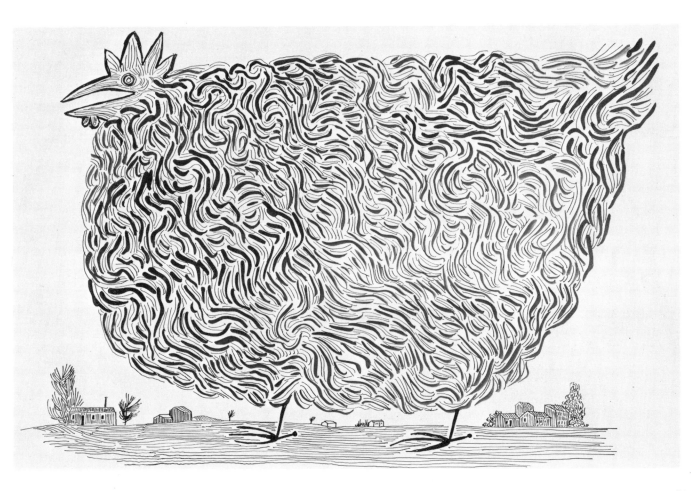

An array of materials used for ink drawing projects.

Ink Drawing Demonstration and Projects

Ink is a very versatile medium which can be used in a variety of ways to produce different effects. In addition to the familiar techniques using ink with brush and pen, there are creative new methods of combining ink with other media, such as crayons and pastels, and making collages in which ink drawing is added to graphic cutouts from magazines and other printed materials.

Two ink projects are illustrated in step-by-step detail in this chapter. They begin on page 54 and show how the artist and student can use ink by itself and in combination with other media. To introduce the two projects, an illustration of tools is given on the opposite page.

Page 54. Simple ink drawing. The Black Count's figure is drawn from the imagination, using the basic materials of India ink, a large brush, and a crowquill pen. After the main shape has been delineated with the brush, fine pen lines are added to create a contrast in texture to the black area with representational details. A variation of this technique might be to contrast ink washes with crowquill pen lines.

Page 56. Ink-collage project. Pieces of paper were brushed with black ink to establish general shapes and then cut with pinking shears. The cutout shapes were glued onto a sheet of white paper. Details were added with a small brush and fine pen and oil crayons to create the black bird. Instead of created inked-and-cutout forms; printed shapes from magazines could be cut out and extended.

I The Black Count

1. A large brush and black ink are used freely to begin an imaginative figure.

2. After the main shape of the figure is brushed in, a crow-quill pen is used to draw fine lines for contrast.

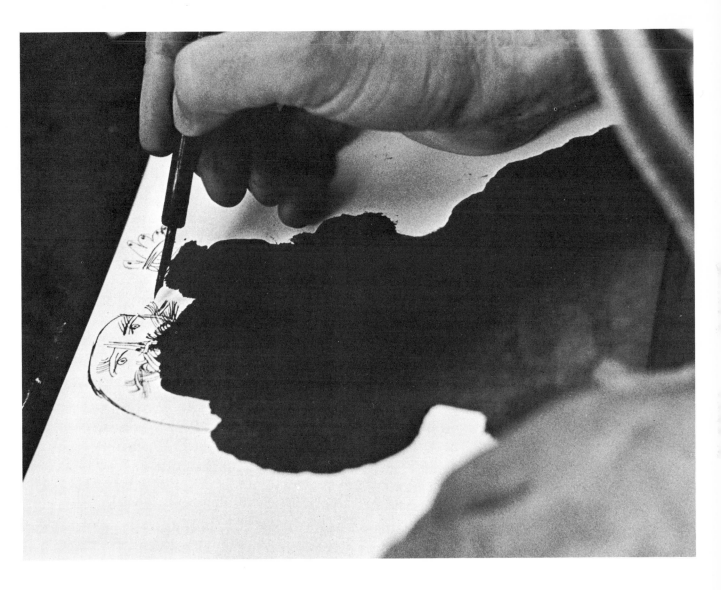

3. The drawing is finished by adding details to the face and hand.

II   The Black Bird

1. Basic shapes are drawn on paper with a large brush and black ink.

2. When the ink is dry, pinking scissors are use to cut out black shapes from the ink forms.

3. The cut shapes are glued onto a sheet of white paper with rubber cement.

4. Details are added to the cut out, glued shapes with a small brush and fine line pen.

5. White oil crayon lines are drawn on top of the black paper shapes.

6. A gray ink wash is brushed around the figure to relieve the tension of too-much black.

7. The finished drawing shows the combination of cut shapes, pen lines, oil crayons, and ink washes.

Page 60

Chicken by Norman Laliberté. Gray washes of varying intensities were brushed on quickly to cover the entire sheet of paper. While the washes were still damp, a small brush laden with black ink was used to define form. A razor blade was then used to scrape the wet gray area, creating a soft line. When dry, a dry brush was used on top of the grays to achieve further textures. The final step was the use of a large brush and black ink to define the drawing more accurately. By superimposing gray upon gray, a wide variety of texture is achieved.

…by Norman Laliberté. Heavy black ink brush drawing with additional pen and ink detail is combined with letters cut out of magazine pages and pasted on top of the drawing.

A Stone Age drawing from the Lascaux Caves in France. It is believed that early man gave graphic expression to his thoughts by using the charred end of sticks or branches as drawing instruments. In effect, this would be the earliest use of a very primitive form of charcoal. (Reproduced courtesy of Musée de l'Homme, Paris.)

PASTEL, CHARCOAL, AND CHALK DRAWING

Early History of Pastel, Charcoal, and Chalk

Pastel, charcoal, and chalk—in varying forms of manufacture — have been used by artists and architects for centuries.

Pastel, a dry powder pigment with a minimum of non-greasy binder, was first used extensively in portraiture, notably by Chardin (1699-1779), Nattier (1685-1766), LaTour (1704-1788), and others. It provided the artist with a method of drawing in a full range of color without the usual waiting required for drying.

When rubbed or stroked against the paper, the pastel stick shatters or disintegrates to very fine powdered particles which adhere to the paper with a soft, almost feathery quality. But this same softness, which is the finest attribute of the pastel, is also its greatest weakness, for it lends itself much too readily to accidental smudging.

Soft pastels can be used as effectively as paint or watercolor in covering a complete surface with a wide range of color. It was this quality that made it popular as an early medium for portraits. Pastels are also made with rigid or harder substances which readily lend themselves to drawing and to producing work with linear and sketch effects. This latter form of pastel found extensive use with early artists for making preliminary studies preparatory to a major work. Edgar Degas (1834-1917) used pastels in both these ways and, in addition, developed a number of new techniques to give his work permanence and greater beauty.

Primitive man is believed to have executed some of the early cave pictures by using charred sticks or twigs as drawing instruments, but in the civilized era charcoal was first used by draftsmen who found in it qualities helpful to early architectural expression.

Charcoal, in its original form, has little adhesive power. Manufactured from split willow sticks, it is a brittle substance which was used by early artists as a preliminary sketching tool, for it could be erased from canvas or paper almost at will. Later, linseed oil was added to the manufacturing process of artists' charcoal to give the medium (while it was still fresh) a deep or rich black adhesive quality. Jacopo Tintoretto (1518-1594) and Giacomo Cavedoni (1577-1660) were among the early artists to make extensive use of the medium in this latter form.

Most drawing media have a tendency to mark or adhere to the high part of the paper.

Charcoal seems to recline in the hollows of the surface and this, of course, gives importance to the selection of the paper on which the medium is to be used. Charcoal manufactured with oil will leave a grease trail or shadow on either side of the line it produces, which at times gives added effect to the composition.

Chalk, a fine-grained and soft limestone substance, has been known as a writing or marking instrument throughout a number of periods in history, having been formed naturally in many parts of the world during the earth's Cretaceous period. Chalk was extensively used by early artists of northern Europe when panel paintings coated with white gesso were highly popular. It is also a vital ingredient in oil grounds which form the basis of many paint substances.

Prior to the time of manufactured chalk and other fabricated drawing media, the adhesive quality of black, natural chalk had popular usage and was used extensively for studying details (and for practicing figure drawing) in Renaissance and post-Renaissance times. Cennino Cennini, the Italian painter and writer, wrote of drawing with chalk in the 14th century. Red chalk was used by Leonardo da Vinci (1452-1519), and black chalk was used by artists on blue paper at the beginning of the 16th century.

Later in that century, artists began to use combinations of red, black, and white chalks on blue paper to achieve a greater range of color within their compositions and to give their work a greater sense of dimension.

Frequently in describing the work of artists of earlier time, there is some confusion between crayon drawing and drawing with the pastel, charcoal, and chalk media. This is because manufacturing processes (stemming from a desire to improve and extend the qualities of natural drawing materials) were in a period of discovery and development and because the French word *crayon* originally was commonly used in describing a great variety of drawing media, including the graphite or lead pencil and sticks of pastel. In our time, we use the word "crayon" for solid substances which have a wax or oil binder; "pastel" for a medium which has no binder (or very little binder) and which is manufactured in a range of values within a given color; "chalk" for a drawing commodity which has a non-greasy or non-oil binder in a number of colors without a specific range of values within a given color; and cased drawing instruments (frequently wood) which are popularly known as "color pencils."

Still Life with Glass, Fruit Dish and Knife (1927) by Georges Braque (1882-1963). The quality of this pastel composition is extremely soft and almost velvet-like in appearance. (Reproduced courtesy of The Art Institute of Chicago, Potter Palmer Collection.)

Master and Contemporary Pastel, Charcoal, and Chalk Drawings

This chapter includes drawings in pastel, charcoal, and chalk media by contemporary artists. During the first half of this century, to some people drawing in pastel became identified with sentiment, and sentiment in turn denoted weakness. Many of the examples shown here completely shatter this concept, for they cover a great many techniques that bring forth qualities of strength, effervescence, textural impression, and much vitality.

In commenting on the potentiality of the pastel medium, Beatrice Thompson(page 75) notes "...It is one of the best and most inspiring introductions to the elements of drawing and painting. The student feels an immediate excitement; drawing with color does not produce the fear or require the specialized skill that painting does, and the feeling of control, along with the sensuous brilliance of the colors, becomes a real impetus for the imagination. The effects that can be achieved are manifold, as it encompasses drawing as well as introducing the student to some of the techniques of painting... The student's experience in juxtaposing, mixing, and overlaying color is a valuable preparation for the difficulties of painting."

As the examples here illustrate, contemporary artists working in pastel, charcoal, and chalk have been able to achieve for these media the acceptance of being full-fledged master drawings in themselves. They are both searching and subtle, in instances intimate and sensitive, and always represent a deep personal statement by the artist. They represent the concepts and ideas of their makers, they convey observations and reflections, they are as deliberate or as spontaneous as life itself.

Picasso, Cassatt, Breverman, de Kooning, Dubuffet, Hartung and others — here are both vignettes and milestones of life recorded for history through the use of the pastel, charcoal, and chalk media. As important as *what* has been drawn is *how* it has been drawn: the spirit, the strength, the sensitivity with which the subject has been rendered. And in this respect, pastel, charcoal, and chalk have special individual attributes and qualities of which the artist, through varying techniques, can make full and outstanding use.

Speaking of drawing, René Huyghe of the Académie Française has observed that "Of all the creative acts performed by the artist, the most directly legible is drawing. Drawing is also the first to which the artist resorts when he sketches the future form of what is still a mere feeling within himself. Finally, it is the act that is most directly and spontaneously governed by his nervous and muscular system."

Because they are quick, dry, expressive, colorful, and immediate, pastel, charcoal, and chalk are among the most responsive of media for the transformation of idea to reality.

Woman and Flowers (1937) by Henri Matisse (1869-1954). This heavy charcoal drawing has an equal line quality throughout. Gray is used to create textures in both the vase and the head and seems to have been created by rubbing or smudging from the black charcoal line. (Reproduced courtesy of the Joseph Hirshhorn Foundation, photo by Geoffrey Clements.)

Portrait of George Limbour by Jean Dubuffet. Although this is a serious charcoal portrait by a great artist, there is still a child-like quality to the composition. The small body has a very large head and the arms extend beyond the normal proportion of the figure. Note the deliberate use of the paper texture to create dark and light effects. (Reproduced courtesy of Pierre Matisse Gallery, New York, photo by Eric Pollitzer.)

Seated Woman No. 1 by Willem de Kooning. This pastel drawing may well be compared with *Muscular Dynamism* by Umberto Boccioni on page 33, not from the point of view of movement but in the way both the figures and the space have been exploded. The viewer is conscious that the de Kooning composition represents one figure, but that its elements have yet to be brought together or united. Some areas of the drawing have been scratched to allow the gray to come through the black. Black chalk has been dragged over the other areas to create an out-of-focus impression. (Reproduced courtesy of Mr. and Mrs. Sherman H. Star, Lexington, Mass., photo by Barney Burstein.)

Opposite Page

The Dancers, 1899, by Edgar Degas (1834–1917). Degas as a master of chalk, charcoal, and pastel gave his compositions in these media uncanny qualities of light and textural feeling. In this study, the figures are more than defined by the pastel; they actually appear to be molded by the medium. (Reproduced courtesy of the Toledo Museum of Art, gift of Edward Drummond Libbey, 1928.)

Clowns et Personnages by Georges Seurat (1859-1891). This charcoal composition is greatly affected by the almost incredible use of the texture of the paper on which it is drawn. The four figures depicted appear to be rendered in four different ways by Seurat's talented dexterity with the medium. Note that there is a complete absence of detail in the figures — no eyes, no facial features, no buttons on their clothing. They have been universalized. Despite this, however, the viewer is quite aware of their individual personality as projected fully and forcefully. Seurat regarded mastery of drawing as a prerequisite for painting and produced hundreds of drawings of which a great many are considered to be masterpieces in themselves.

Opposite Page

Les Saltimbanques (1940) by Fernand Léger (1881–1955). Everything in this charcoal drawing is round and spherical in shape, and a multiplicity of shades and shadows prevails throughout the composition. There is a great, even line quality to this work, and the roundness in certain area, achieved by rubbing in the round, gives the entire drawing a bas relief or sculptured appearance. (Private Collection, Mr. and Mrs. Daniel Saidenberg, New York; reproduced with kind permission. Photo by John D. Schiff.)

On a brick-red painted board, charcoal, conte, and white chalk are used together in a figure drawing.

A collage is created by cutting out and pasting sections of drawing. Neutral and colored papers are used, and the different parts of the composition are worked in charcoal, pastel, and conte crayon, respectively. Oil wash is used throughout.

Lioness with Bird (1641) by Rembrandt (1606-1669). A black chalk drawing with white and ink washes. (Reproduced courtesy of the British Museum.)

Teaching Techniques in Pastels, Charcoal, and Conte Crayon
by Beatrice Thompson

As a classroom teacher of drawing, I have found that the media of pastel, charcoal, and conte crayon can serve as remarkably effective introductions to the elements of drawing and painting. For beginning students, drawing with color does not require the same specialized skill that painting does, and the rapid development of a degree of technical control, along with the vivid esthetic qualities of these media, constitute a real impetus to the imagination.

The effects that can be achieved with pastel, charcoal, and conte are manifold. Through precisely limited problems, I explore the following: structural line drawing; contrast of textures; developing masses by crosshatching and by the rubbing smooth of flat planes; space, volume, and modeling; light and shadow; two-dimensional drawing and pattern. Tough-textured papers help to break the harshness of line with granular effects implying light and atmosphere. Color can be blended by rubbing, by the overlaying of small strokes, and by wetting the drawing to form a unifying pale wash.

In this chapter I record the assignments given during a single drawing course (a semester or a year), and the examples, which illustrate the teaching sequence, have been taken from both high-school and college levels. The problems go from beginning to advanced stages and are analyzed in a step-by-step procedure. Captions accompanying illustrations contain details related to techniques and materials involved in each problem.

Before the students undertake a complete problem and attempt finished work, I demonstrate certain qualities and effects of the media, presenting exercises and commenting on master drawings. I use drawings by Leonardo, Rubens, and Watteau to emphasize linear form; the color is limited, and the accents are made in white or black. I also use works by Degas, Seurat, Cassatt, Moreau, Redon, and Picasso. Degas worked in overlaid, divided strokes for effects of light, depth, and contrast; Redon and Moreau brought pastel drawing close to stained-glass effects by using flat tones rubbed to a jewel-like intensity.

Under close guidance, the students perform exercises embodying some of these techniques and then go on to full-scale drawing assignments.

The teacher will need to order the following supplies: a box of pastels for each student; compressed charcoal; red and white conte crayons; two chamois cloths for each student; one for charcoal and one for red conte; a few tubes of oil paints to be shared by students; medium yellow, yellow ochre, ultramarine blue, burnt siena, burnt umber, cadmium red, black; a 1-inch hardware brush and a No. 11 watercolor brush for each student; a can of gesso; charcoal papers in white and different pale colors; chipboard to be covered with a ground of paint or gesso; colored papers for collage construction.

A group of works in different media exemplify a range of drawing techniques that are incorporated into classroom problems using pastels, charcoal, and conte crayon.

1. Detail of *The Angel Appearing to the Shepherds* by Rembrandt. This etching is a brilliant example of the power of crosshatching to create effects of spatial complexity and texture. (Reproduced courtesy of The Metropolitan Museum of Art, gift of George Coe Graves, the Sylmaris Collection, 1920.)

2. *Extravaganza of Balance* by Francisco Goya. Another etching embodies a careful juxtaposition of dark, middle, and light values and also textural changes from smooth to linear to modeled form. The bold silhouetting of the horse and figure shows the student a useful method of dramatizing an image within a complex picture. (The Metropolitan Museum of Art, Rogers Fund, 1919.)

3

4

3. *Battle Scene* by Peter Paul Rubens. In this pen and ink wash drawing with gouache, an overall medium value is accented by dark line, and volume is emphasized by the use of white. A similar effect can be achieved using conte, charcoal, and white chalk. (Reproduced courtesy of The Metropolitan Museum of Art, Gustavus A. Pfeiffer Fund, 1964.)

4. *Portrait of an Unknown Man* by Jean Auguste Ingres. A pencil drawing combines a variety of linear effects. The face is modeled in great detail, while the hair and garment are lightly sketched with few accents. Later problems in this chapter show this technique as adapted by students in charcoal and conte. (Reproduced courtesy of The Metropolitan Museum of Art, Rogers Fund, 1919.)

Beginning Problems–Pastel

1. *The Bather* by Edgar Degas. Basing drawing
assignments on the style of this Degas drawing in
pastels, I point out the rich overlays of contrasting
colors, and direct the students to work in vertical
lines (horizontal lines can also be used effectively).
The limitation of linear form provides a framework
within which the beginning student explores essential
qualities of the medium. (Reproduced courtesy of The
Metropolitan Museum of Art. The H.O. Havemeyer
Collection, bequest of Mrs. H.O. Havemeyer, 1929.)

1

2

3

4

2. The first assignment is designed to introduce students to the basic elements of color, texture, and line quality. Subject matter is kept fairly simple, comprising a single figure or head, a floral still life, or a plant with several objects. The problem calls for the use of vertical lines only, varying in length and width, and there is no rubbing of surfaces. Images are defined by a simple outline or by the articulation of negative space around them. The student concentrates on the subtlety and richness he can develop through the extensive layering of individual strokes and different colors. Related to the impressionist technique of broken color, this practice results in a remarkable depth of tone and produces a vivid interplay of subtle shades. Such a problem can also be executed using colored papers to provide a basic tone and a point of departure for effects of line. Also, each layer of strokes can be sprayed with fixative in order to prevent smudging; this way of creating definite levels leads to an extraordinary composite effect of color and texture. Another interesting variation of the problem calls for an initial layer of one color only, covering the entire page in strokes of different sizes. The images are first defined by a very faint outline; eventually, the outlines disappear as areas are built up by the overlapping of contrasting or related colors to fill out the forms, giving way to a pattern of values.

3. The second assignment embodies the bold and exciting pattern-making potential of the medium. A complete composition is outlined with a very heavy dark or black line, and the areas so defined are filled in with rich solid masses of color that are deepened and varied with overlays and hand-rubbings. Thus, images composed of deep color tones are defined and detailed by the rhythm of a dominant line that contracts and expands to form a pattern of panel-like units, resembling the effect of stained-glass. The bounding line can also be drawn in ink with a brush or heavy felt-tip pen.

4. Omitting the outline, colors are applied in the same way as above and rubbed in layers to fuse the forms together; where accents are desired hard edges can be created with color-masses alone.

Advanced Problems in Pastel

1. Advanced problems should present technical
elaborations as means of achieving greater stylistic
interest. The objects in a composition are first defined
with a faint outline. In a single color, long parallel
diagonal lines are used to silhouette the forms; lines
of the same color and configuration fill in the
background, which is differentiated by an overall
contrast of line width. The use of a single color
furnishes a basic tone for the composition and helps
to guide the student as he builds up further layers of
changing color. After the paper is fully covered with
lines of one color, a second layer of lines roughly
parallel to the first combines a variety of colors to
further define the imagery and to develop volume
with systematic value contrasts. Without rubbing by
hand, many layers of color are added, and the lines
continue to vary in thickness and length. The result is
a valuable exploration of line-and-depth effects, with
textural force enhancing a richness of color that is
organized by dramatic value patterns.

2. Another advanced problem deals with
crosshatching. A single line is used to outline the
parts of the drawing and the basic details of the
composition. Parallel diagonal lines of various
lengths cover the areas in different colors, and the
picture as a whole incorporates a range of color and
value contrasts. Many layers of lines are added, each
layer composed of parallel lines that cross the lines of
the previous layer at a narrow angle. Without rubbing, the surface is built up to great complexity; the
crosshatched lines themselves can produce the effect
of rubbing. The background is developed
simultaneously with the central images.

3. In variations of the advanced problem, lines may be limited to 1/8- or 1/4-inch lengths; the background may be fused in places with foreground images, with some areas accented by brilliant hard edges. Color may be limited as follows: a basic contrast of dull background surrounding bright objects; the entire picture composed in related colors, using a full gradation of values; a whole scheme of dull colors in a range of values. Pale pastel can be rubbed in masses by hand to give the effect of a wash; specific areas are then defined by heavily crosshatched lines.

Advanced Problems in Charcoal and Conte Crayon

1. An advanced problem begins with the first four steps used in the last set of problems (beginning techniques). A rich velvety surface is built up with numerous layers of charcoal or conte, rubbed by hand and with chamois, and strong light-and-dark contrasts are developed throughout the composition. An eraser is used to achieve textural effects; the student repeatedly erases, reworks, and erases again over the same area. Parallel and crosshatched lines add further contrast. This problem gives the student an appreciation of the strong dramatic potential of these media and combines techniques of line drawing and painterly layering in a powerful chiaroscuro treatment.

2. A variation of the advanced problem calls for the fusing and blurring of certain images into the dark background, creating a *sfumato* effect. Also, the background may be divided equally into light and dark areas; silhouetted in line, the foreground images in each half of the picture can be made to contrast with their background.

3. A red conte drawing is based on a portrait by Ingres. Using drawing techniques, students work on interpretive translations of master paintings.

4. In another variation of the advanced problem, the lighter values may be heightened by the use of white chalk or conte.

The Planting of the Flag.
White pastel was applied very
lightly over smooth, black
paper. Gray pastel was then
added on top of the white, and
a razor blade was used to
scratch out details of the figure.

Double Head. A soft charcoal pencil drawing on heavy textured paper. The gray wash was achieved by using water on the residue from the pencil point on the paper.

Pastel, Charcoal, and Chalk Drawings
by Norman Laliberté

In this chapter, artist Norman Laliberté applies his imagination and energetic efforts to drawing in the pastel, charcoal, and chalk media. The caption accompanying each rendering describes in detail the various techniques Laliberté employs in creating a composition and the effect which these methods achieve. Laliberté's thoughts and concepts are forerunners to the techniques he experiments with and uses and are recorded, in part, as follows:

"An artist is himself, no matter what. Whether he paints or uses pastels and chalk, whether he is eating, walking or just meditating, he is himself, unlike anyone else. The action of painting or of drawing — the actual doing it — most often takes away from his art of creation. . .that is the action of provoking to the mind new ideas which were not there previously.

"Art is the rendering of an idea. . .the giving of form, of shape, of body to the idea. The important part of the creation is to have the idea. While doing the art, you are in a sense a slave to the idea. The next creation starts when the actual work is completed . . . the next idea . . . the next drawing.

"To an artist, aesthetics are more than the technique. The way the thing looks is really an accident to the concept. It's an added gift in a sense. I am not sure that artists are trying to paint beauty; they do what they have to, and the beauty or the sense of proportion or the design or the color somewhat follows, mostly accidentally.

"In a sense all art must be a sacrifice, a sacrifice of all the other ideas which have to be abandoned. You must make the work explicit, make it understood in order to communicate. The way you feel about a certain object or person, your real feelings about it, may be too personal to be understood. Something is always left behind: a color, a shade, a line, using a symbol to symbolize something else, a bird in the sky to show freedom or flight, a flower to show tenderness or growth. Even then, what kind of bird? What kind of flower? I mean, you may put in a bird or a flower — but not all of them or even as many as you would like to. You simply can't put in all the birds and all the flowers of the universe. You just can't put in enough, and that is the sacrifice.

"No matter what you discover or think, you can only communicate it on a certain level, anyway. There is simply no way of saying or of communicating everything you have in mind. You keep on trying to invent new ways of expressing yourself. Sometimes you find a new way. . .you evolve a different technique or find a new material with which to work, and it turns out that you get further away from communicating with your audience than closer, which was your original intent. What is more important is your own honest reaction at first and then the reaction of your critic. Of course, we are not pure spirit, and there must be some understanding of the media and the method. . .

"About the drawings for this book? It's in us, and we have to put it down in some form, somewhere."

Brown paper was ripped very loosely and pasted down onto a white background. Very heavy black chalk was used to define the ripped edge of the paper and to create its own textured line. Black paper was ripped and pasted down to form facial features. Further details were added with white pastel.

Detail from:
Punch and Judy. A heavy-toothed black paper was used for the background in this drawing. Chalk was applied very lightly to form the two figures. Soft white pastel was then applied over the chalk drawing to add details such as the hat, eyes, and flowers.

Portrait panel from a mummy. Encaustic
on wood panel. Egypt, 2nd century A.D.
(The Metropolitan Museum of Art,
New York, gift of Edward S. Harkness,
1917-1918.)

Funeral portrait from Faiyum, Egypt.
Encaustic on wood. 2nd century A.D.
(The Metropolitan Museum of Art,
New York, Rogers Fund, 1909.)

PAINTING WITH CRAYONS

Early History of Wax and Crayons

ENCAUSTIC

The simple crayon as we know it today may owe its ancestry to the Egyptians of some 3,000 years B.C., who are believed to have painted on stone by employing a type of encaustic—or hot wax—method. Pigments were mixed with refined beeswax, sometimes with oils or resins, and a "burning-in" process was applied when the painting was completed. This was achieved by passing heat over the finished surface, thereby internally wedding the paint into a solid state, without damaging or melting the face of the picture.

The Greeks of about 350 B.C. were known to have used wax mixed with tar for caulking: they discovered that color or pigment added to this mixture made possible a crude type of decoration for the prows of their ships that were to take them on voyages of battle and exploration. Before long a modified version of this method was used for decorative expression on walls and panels. One art historian (G.M.A. Richter, *A Handbook of Greek Art,* Phaidon Press Ltd.) attributes the development of encaustic painting at this point to Pausias of Sikian at the beginning of the 4th century B.C., and an example on marble, the fragmentary stelae of Hediste of the 3rd century B.C., exists today in the Museum of Volo, Greece.

At the dawn of the Christian era, the Romans devised an ingenious method for personal communication: tablets of metal or wood coated with a smooth surface of wax on which they wrote with a bone or ivory stylus. But the Egyptians of about 100 A.D. provide the best examples of encaustic painting available to us: the Faiyum mummy portraits. Religious tradition demanded that persons of state be entombed with a portrait of the deceased that would withstand the erosion of time. And well they did, for examples of these encaustic works (painted on wood) are to be seen in a number of museums today, still bright in color, apparently protected by the burning-in process with which they were created and by their smooth, hard wax exterior surfaces. Many Greco-Roman sculptures of the period were coated in wax colors and rubbed to a high polish with cloths. The Romans also used wax as a painting preservative and were known to apply coats of it to decorative surfaces and to frescoes.

Icons executed by the encaustic method of painting in the 6th century A.D. exist today at St. Catherine's monastery in the Sinai Peninsula. The monastery also has examples of mosaics attributed to the 12th century, in which artists created portrait compositions by setting minute cubes of highly polished stone or colored glass known as *tesserae* into a bed of wax, which held them firmly in place.

Self Portrait in crayon
by Oskar Kokoschka
(1923). (Collection, The
Museum of Modern Art,
New York.)

Right, above: Crayon
drawing by Käthe
Kollwitz, from the series
Pictures of Misery.
(Richter Portfolio,
collection of Henry
Ernest, Montreal. Photo
by Hans Trevor Deutsch.)
Below: Two Lawyers.
Crayon and wash
drawing by Honoré
Daumier (1806-1879).
(Courtesy National
Gallery of Art,
Washington, D.C. Gift of
Myron A. Hofer.)

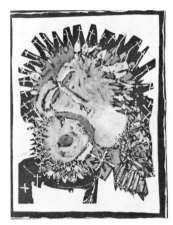

Hodie, print with oil crayon application, by Norman Laliberté.

Master and Contemporary Crayon Works

Because *crayon* in the French language means stick or pencil, drawings in chalk, pastel, pencil and charcoal—as well as in actual crayon—were frequently referred to as crayon drawings in the 18th and 19th centuries. With the emergence of the crayon as a serious art tool in this century, the accepted definition of it is "an uncased solid medium with a binder of fat or wax."

Many of the old masters used a form of fabricated crayon, including sticks of oiled charcoal, for their preliminary drawings. The 16th century Italian painter, Jacopo da Pontormo (1494-1556), who was a student of Leonardo da Vinci, is thought to have used a form of crayon shaded by rubbing to achieve ivory tones on drawings of bones of the human anatomy. Crayon was developed in that century, too, for use by draftsmen and architects, who, without our modern fixatives, sought a drawing tool that would smudge less easily. The French portraitist, Francois Clouet (1520-1572), drew a number of his subjects by applying fine lines and minute dots with red and black crayons.

John Linnell (1792-1882), the English portrait and landscape painter and close friend of William Blake, frequently used crayon as a working medium, and Eugène Delacroix (1798-1863), of the French Romantic era, may well have been thinking of his own facility with the black crayon when he declared that to achieve the status of a true artist a student must first learn to complete a drawing of a man falling off a building, before the unfortunate man hit the ground.

Others to use crayon were Georges Seurat (1859-1891), a French Neo-Impressionist, who achieved notable effects in his drawings by the imaginative use of erasing; Henri Matisse (1869-1954), who perfected the use of the side or broad of the crayon rather than its point; Toulouse-Lautrec (1864-1901), who worked from time to time with wax crayons; and the prolific graphic artist Käthe Kollwitz (1867-1945), who drew some of her original works in crayon. Drawings and paintings executed in this medium are to be found in art schools and galleries, museums and private collections throughout North America.

Above: Boy by Fred Ross.
Wax crayon drawing.
(Photo by Hans Trevor
Deutsch.)

Below: Study for the
*Portrait of James
Tissot* by Edgar Degas.
Black crayon on light
brown paper. (Fogg Art
Museum, Harvard
University, Gift of
C. M. de Hauke.)

Above: Dark Keyhole by
P. K. Irwin. Wax crayon
with sgraffito. (National
Gallery of Canada,
Ottawa.)

Below: Street Children
by Paul Klee. Black
crayon drawing.
(Collection, The Museum
of Modern Art, New York,
Gift of Clifford Odets.)

Nativity, print with oil crayon application, by Norman Laliberté.

Crayon Demonstrations

Although wax and oil crayons are sold almost everywhere, including the dime store, and in spite of their use in virtually every elementary classroom in the country, few artists or teachers have any idea of their amazing potential for creative expression. Crayons can produce the depth of color and brilliance of oils as well as the subtle hues of watercolor and pastel. They can be applied layer upon layer for glazes or, in the case of oil crayons, smeared and blended with the fingers for rich, soft surfaces. Among the unique advantages of crayons are their low cost, ease of handling, and durability. In the hands of the imaginative artist or student, crayons are a serious medium capable of giving form and color to the most sophisticated ideas or decorative schemes. Given encouragement and basic technical instruction, children quickly learn to create works of great intensity and beauty.

The technical notes below and the illustrated demonstrations in this chapter are designed to familiarize the artist and teacher with the basic characteristics of crayons and techniques for using them.

WAX CRAYONS

Wax crayons are, perhaps, the most taken for granted art medium available. They possess, nevertheless, outstanding characteristics, the greatest of which is the uniquely beautiful waxy surface they produce when they are applied with a fair amount of pressure. Worked color over color, they create subtle or brilliant combinations. Wax crayons are ideal for resist paintings. In this technique black or colored inks are brushed over the finished crayon painting, thus saturating all exposed areas of the paper not covered by crayon, which repels the ink. Wax crayons can be successfully combined with many other media as well, including watercolors, thinned acrylic paints, colored dyes, pastels, and pencils.

Sgraffito techniques create beautiful texture and line designs. Crayon can be scratched and scraped to reveal other crayon colors or paper surfaces underneath with any sharp instrument, such as a nail, pin, broken pencil, or razor blade. Wax crayons can also be melted. Interesting translucent designs can be made by placing bits and flakes of colored wax crayons between sheets of wax paper and laminating the paper and crayon "sandwich" together with a warm iron.

OIL CRAYONS

Oil crayons are even more versatile than wax crayons and have a greater color brilliance. Their softer consistency encourages highly expressive thick-and-thin line effects. They can be rubbed with the fingers for transparent smeared areas. Oil crayons can be intermixed on the painting surface for rich color combinations and vibrant glaze passages. Like wax crayons, they can be incised and scraped with any sharp tool at hand. Again like wax crayons, oil crayons can be combined with many other media as examples in the following demonstrations show.

Opposite Page

Black oil crayon drawing on heavy textured cotton.

Particularly beautiful surfaces can be achieved with oil crayons by painting over them with a brush dipped in turpentine. The turpentine partially dissolves the crayon so that it can be brushed much like oil paint. A similar effect results by drawing with oil crayons on paper pre-dampened with turpentine.

SURFACES

Wax and oil crayons can be used successfully on many surfaces. These include any paper (dull, glossy, smooth, textured, colored, white—even tissue paper), cardboard, sandpaper, canvas, fine and coarse fabrics, Masonite, and wood (untreated, waxed or coated with gesso for best results). Crayons can be used directly on most walls for mural projects.

FINISHING TECHNIQUES

Wax crayon paintings can be rubbed to a pleasing light gloss with a soft cloth. For greater gloss, and more durability, they can be protected with a coat of long lasting floor wax.

Oil crayon paintings, particularly those on hard surfaces such as Masonite or wood, are greatly enhanced by a final application of shellac, varnish, or polymer medium (matte or gloss). These increase the natural color brilliance and greatly aid permanence.

DEMONSTRATION

On the following pages Norman Laliberté demonstrates step by step how an oil crayon can be used alone and with a turpentine wash. Wax and watercolor crayon techniques are explored in the following section of this chapter. Techniques can range from linear designs employing a single crayon to the highly textured, detailed surface combining as many as six or seven media with crayons. These are only a few of the ways the student or artist can approach crayon painting. Imagination and experimentation will lead to many more.

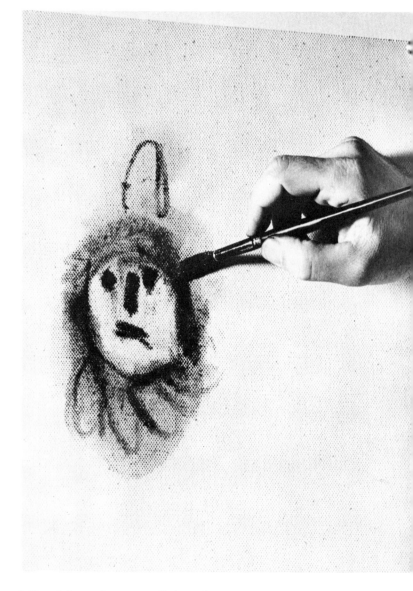

1. The painting surface is an unstretched piece of heavily textured canvas. A brush dipped in turpentine is worked over a preliminary oil crayon drawing. The crayon softens on contact with the turpentine to produce soft, blurred passages.

2. Turpentine is brushed
over the oil crayon
surface for a transparent
watercolor effect.

3. Further application of
oil crayons onto the
damp surface.

4. Because the surface is moist, it is easy to make changes as the painting progresses.

Opposite Page
5. The finished painting, "Cat and Fish." Whiskers were added last by pulling a white oil crayon dipped in turpentine across the surface.

Gloria, print with oil
crayon application, by
Norman Laliberté.

Projects in Oil and Wax Crayons

In addition to individual drawings and paintings, wax and oil crayons are used frequently in a wide array of projects. Some of these include: melting wax crayons and applying them to heavy cardboard with a stiff brush, thus obtaining rich and luminous effects; achieving a painted appearance by the use of crayon with a turpentine wash; etching by using crayon on crayon or paint on crayon; the use of tempera wash over a partially wax-crayoned picture; crayon drawings on sandpaper or other textured surfaces; and laminating by using wax crayon flakes or chips pressed with a warm iron between two sheets of heavy wax paper, thus producing a transparent stained-glass effect.

This section shows a number of projects done with oil and wax crayons. These include the enrichment of a large photostated design achieved by color highlighting only certain portions of the photostat, thus creating an effective contrast; examples of oil crayon on wood, including mounted crayoned cutouts to give the effect of three dimensions; simple games created by applying crayon on wood, and examples of what is perhaps the most popular of all wax or oil crayon projects in many schools and art classes—the multi-colored group mural.

Opposite Page
A photograph of an
architectural detail is
photostated and enlarged.
The insert is then
decorated with oil crayon.

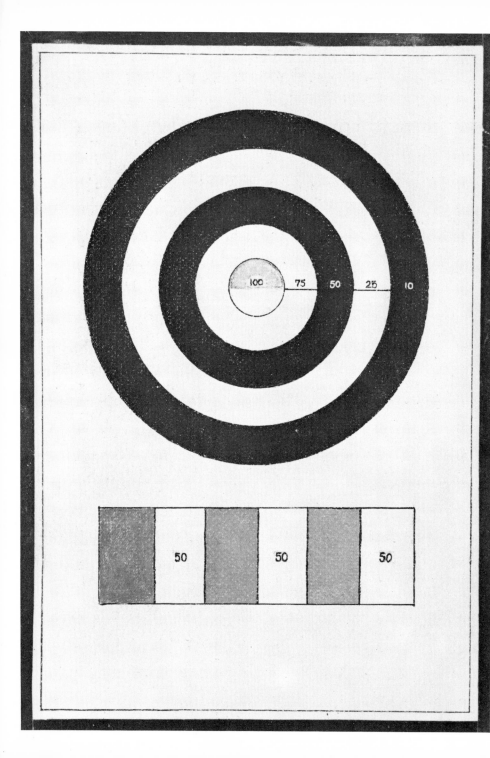

Above: Soldier. A collage
by Push Pin Studios, Inc.
Embellishment extension
of a drawing with crayon
by Anne Raymo.

Left: Target. Crayon
on composition board by
Karen Brown.

Ancient music box
decorated with oil crayon
and shellac. (Photo
by Thecla.)

Left: Oil crayon on heavy
pine panel, 2 by 8 feet.
Right: Detail of panel.
(Photos by Thecla.)

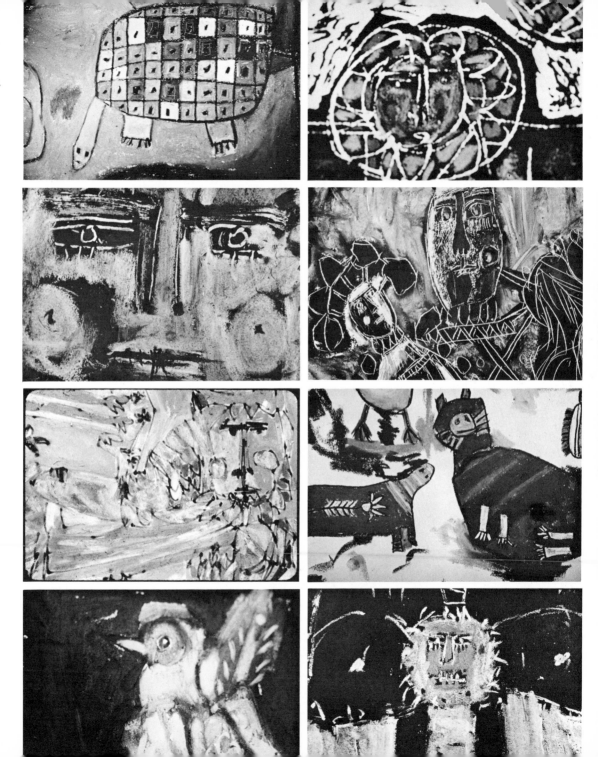

An array of oil crayon drawings by Norman Laliberté on textured papers, using various materials and surfaces.

Extending the perimeter of a picture. A small photograph or illustration is pasted onto a sheet of drawing paper and the child is encouraged to extend the background, foreground, and surroundings as he imagines them.

Solomon's Song of Songs,
two views by Bill Greer.
Wax crayons, dyes, and
concentrated inks, incor-
porating resist technique.

The Sun Bird. Oil crayons were applied leaving a number of open white areas. India ink washes were applied over the oil crayon and the drawing was defined and detailed by scratching and adding gray crayon.

Top left: Title Page.
Top right: Deck of Cards.
Bottom left: The Juggler.
Bottom right: The High Priestess. Drawings based on the French Tarot playing cards which were painted for Charles VI in 1392.

Examples of oil crayon on redwood by Norman Laliberté. Figures are cut out with a bandsaw and inside details are incised with a drill. A coat of shellac or varnish finishes the figure with a rich quality. (Photo by Thecla.)

Nativity Scene. The mural is 4 by 8 feet and executed with the broad side of the crayon to give a broken line effect. Oil crayon on paper.

Opposite Page
Murals depicting the Crusades, by Joan Pearson, St. Mary's College, Notre Dame, Indiana. The gigantic task of drawing literally hundreds of yards of illustrations was completed by Miss Pearson within a period of three months. (Photographs by Ernie Borror.)

Mural by the students
of the Art Department of
Webster College,
St. Louis, Missouri.

Murals by the students
of the Art Department
of Newton College of the
Sacred Heart,
Newton, Mass.

Les mots en liberté futuristes by F.T. Marinetti (1909). Experimentation in all directions by artists, architects, musicians, and writers was prevalent during the early 20th century; the wide experimentation in the graphic arts was strongly influenced by the Dada movement. Almost arbitrarily, artists cut out images from magazines and newspapers and pasted them down in various shapes, positions, and patterns producing a type of collage revolutionary for its time.

COLLAGE, MONTAGE, AND ASSEMBLAGE

Early History of Collage

As periodicals and newspapers became readily available, the art of collage as a folk activity emerged first in Europe and then in America. Its origin can be traced back through the centuries — examples exist of pictures and designs created by pasting together bits and pieces of printed pages to express simple or sentimental compositions and ornamental or decorative themes.

Handmade valentines, paper cutouts and paste-ons, tinsel pictures, scrapbooks (containing product labels, wrappers, pieces of printed advertising, souvenirs, and mementos), screens, vases, and bowls decorated through the use of pasted-on elements — all these are vestiges of collage as an American folk art in the 19th century.

Earlier, Dutch and Flemish artists of the 16th century had produced a number of still-life paintings which deceived the eye with lottery tickets, cards, and torn papers that appeared to be so real that the viewer was tempted to touch them. Raphael Peale, John Peto, and William Harnett were among those artists who continued in this vein in the 1800s.

Finally, during the early 1900s, collage became a form of serious artistic expression as a consequence of the pioneering works of Braque and Picasso. In 1890 Picasso pasted a headline cut from a newspaper onto one of his ink drawings, making it a vital and relevant part of the composition. Almost simultaneously, Georges Braque was experimenting with painted imitations of type and numerals in his compositions, and then began to cut and paste these elements onto the paintings. Very probably the camera contributed to the rapid emergence of the collage as a serious art medium. Picasso, Braque, and other collage artists — Gris, Delaunay, Severini, Boccioni, Arp, Citroën, Ernst, Schwitters — seemed to be saying that the camera had precluded the necessity for creating naturalistic art. What they were attempting was not a denial of real subject matter but, instead, a deep, minutely analytical search to find vital meanings and new values within it.

Quite suddenly, challenging possibilities became evident. No longer could creative urgencies be fulfilled through the techniques of painting on a single plane alone. Space and aspects of the artist's life and personal environment (as reflected through his sensitivities and perceptions) became a cogent part of the composition as materials of many varieties and textures were incorporated and integrated within paintings. The long-standing barriers between painting and sculpture were disintegrating, opening the way to the collage, montage, assemblage, and construction — the new and volatile art forms of an exciting, albeit frightening age.

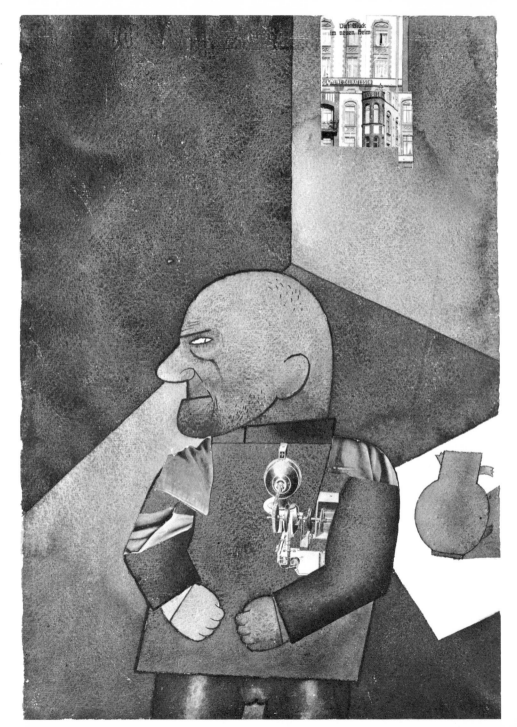

The Engineer Heartfield by George Grosz (1920). A satirical collage in which the artist appears to have cut up and reassembled his own watercolor, adding parts of cities and mechanical objects clipped from magazines to complete the collage. (Reproduced courtesy The Museum of Modern Art, New York. Gift of A. Conger Goodyear.)

Musical Forms by Georges Braque (1918). In this collage the artist has created his subject matter through pasting up paper forms and painting lines over the composition. The serious and classical treatment gives the work the appearance of a finished painting. (Reproduced courtesy the Philadelphia Museum of Art, Louise and Walter Arensberg Collection.)

The Guitar by Pablo Picasso (1926). This collage exemplifies Picasso's greatness; playfully combining a leaf, a piece of string, and several quick lines, he has depicted a lyrical guitar and created a highly poetic composition.

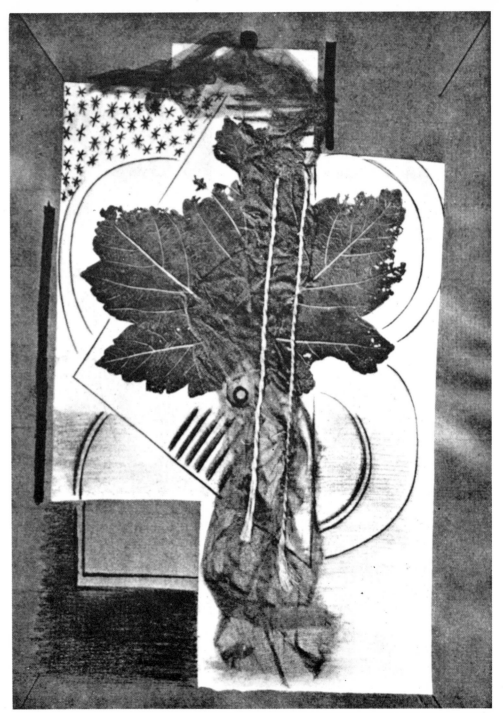

Personnage by Jean Dubuffet (1954). Newspaper cuttings and a black ink line around the figure produce a whimsical, puppet-like character.

Pony Express by Robert Watts (1960-61). An assemblage of wood, steel, polyethylene, brass, glass, a motor, switches and light bulbs. The artist has utilized a small electric motor to activate a brittle construction reflecting elements of America. The outside of a Coca-Cola crate has been covered with pages from a Pony Express account; movement of the horses is the recurring motif of the assemblage, while the flashing lights create an aura of Coney Island. (Courtesy Nationalmuseum, Stockholm.)

Greek Coin. Part of the coin illustration was cut out and pasted onto paper. The illustration was extended and continued with fine brush and ink drawing. Washes were applied within the drawing itself.

Detail of *Altarpiece* by Norman Laliberté.

Contemporary Collage, Montage, and Assemblage

The collage, montage, and assemblage of today constitute statements of the human experience in the second half of the 20th century. The kinds of materials employed are limited only by the artist's imagination.

When the concept of collage was new, pieces of printed papers, product wrappers, stamps, wallpaper, ticket stubs, graphics, letters, numerals, and cloth materials were among the principal elements employed. Generally they were unified with work in another medium on a flat background. Contemporary collages and montages embrace almost every substance known to man: paper, cardboard, wood, glass, metal, plastic, rubber, canvas, cloth, linoleum, neon, bone, burlap, leather, plaster; natural materials like birchbark, leaves, or butterflies; nylon, and even bread and cookies. Though a good many of these are on a flat surface, almost as many are multi-dimensional, and frequently the nature of the materials used determines the composition's shape.

The techniques employed are as varied and as imaginative as the materials themselves. A number of artists cut up their paintings, rearrange some of the elements, and add objects to create their composition. Others, much in the style of the collage originators, unify and provide an environment for pasted-on found objects by drawing or painting in oils, ink, pencil, pastel, charcoal or watercolor. In a number of instances, actual items will represent themselves in the composition—buttons will serve as buttons, and medals will be medals. But a series of ticket stubs might serve as the plumage of a bird, or the works of a watch could represent the mechanism of the brain. Imagination and creativity need not have formality, rhyme or reason.

The collage, assemblage, montage, and construction tell many different things about today. Never has art fulfilled this function more forcefully than through the thought-provoking, introspective collage technique.

The work of Louise Nevelson represents another kind of modern assemblage artist, one who uses found objects as if they were paints produced by a factory. Her objects are the odd shapes, forms, and pieces found on the furniture factory floor—wooden balls and discs, posts, dowels, chunks of patterned molding.

Usually her composition or construction emerges in a series of boxes or compartments. Sprayed or painted in one color, each box represents a comprehensive study in itself, for the parts and pieces have been assembled with precision, depth, and an overwhelming poetic sculptural ability.

Scenes from life (or still life) are the themes of many modern assemblage and construction artists. These are compelling because many times the viewer has the feeling of being drawn into the scene and the lives of the people the objects served.

Joseph Cornell's work extends the medium into a series of beautiful boxes which, while amidst reality, convey a sense of the universe and a life yet to come. His work embraces many different themes—astrology, medicine, science, knowledge and learning, nature— arranged in a spirit that evokes nostalgia, romanticism, and, many times, loneliness.

A single chapter, or a single book for that matter, cannot hope to present the work of all the major artists who today work in the collage, montage, assemblage and construction media. What follows are some outstanding examples which say much about the era when they were created and about the direction toward which art in general, and the collage medium in particular, will journey in the future.

The Surge (detail) by Corrado di Marca-Relli, oil and collage on canvas. The artist mounted individual cut pieces of canvas onto another flat canvas surface. He then proceeded to paint on and around the mounted pieces, thus creating a play and a relationship between the background and the pieces that form his composition. (Reproduced courtesy The Cleveland Museum of Art, Contemporary Collection.)

Photo-montage by Ray K. Metzker. The artist has used fragments of various negatives over and over again to create a new entity and entirely new effect. (Reproduced from *The Persistence of Vision*, Horizon Press, New York, in collaboration with The George Eastman House, Rochester, N.Y.)

Scarecrow, a photo from *55 Vogelflecheuchen* by Hannes Jähn. Examples of montage and assemblage can be found in many unusual places, including farm fields. The scarecrow is a case in point; it is a collection of various materials assembled for a practical use, and yet it has aesthetic value because of the kind of items which were put together, the way in which they were assembled, and the effect that weather has had on the color and texture of materials used.

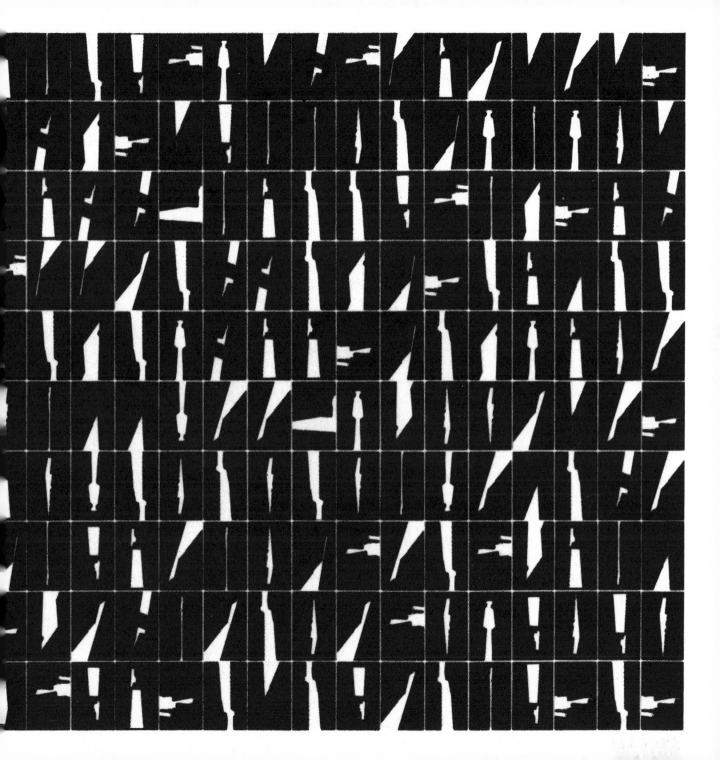

Box Collage by Eliot Hubbard. The old tintype photographs, the worn flag which appears to have flown for a century, the clock and its ancient numerals, and the aged quality of the box that holds these objects combine to give the viewer a trip into nostalgia and to create a montage fragment of American history. (Reproduced with the permission of the Botolph Group, Boston.)

South Carolina Fall by Robert Rauschenberg (1961). In this three-dimensional assemblage, objects have been mounted almost at random, one within another; painting has been added over the objects. Everyday, man-made objects make up this assemblage; they appear ancient because of use, misuse, and altering by present day society. (Courtesy Giuseppe Pauza Si Biurno, Milan. Photograph by Mario Perotti.)

Bed by Robert Rauschenberg (1955). At first glance this work looks like a painting, but upon closer examination the viewer sees the actual fabrics used for the bedspread and pillowcases. Paint has been used heavily on some sections in order to drip onto the neighboring areas; other sections have been left completely unpainted. (Courtesy of Mr. and Mrs. Leo Castelli, Leo Castelli Gallery, New York. Photo by Rudolph Burckhardt.)

Habitat Group for a Shooting Gallery
by Joseph Cornell (1943). Because they
are encased in the box, the birds become
an intimate, very personal kind of art
within themselves. The smashed glass
— as if a shot has taken place — is
used most effectively in steering the
viewer's eye into the box. (Reproduced
courtesy Irving Blum, Los Angeles.)

Opposite Page

Assemblage by Louise Nevelson. Wooden
objects, shapes, and forms — many of
them found in wood-working factories —
have been arranged one within the other
to create an assemblage of spectacular
proportion. The work is usually painted
in one color, and dimension is added by
light flowing into the room. The viewer's
impression of this assemblage depends
on the proximity and angle at which it is
seen. (Courtesy Pace Gallery, New
York.)

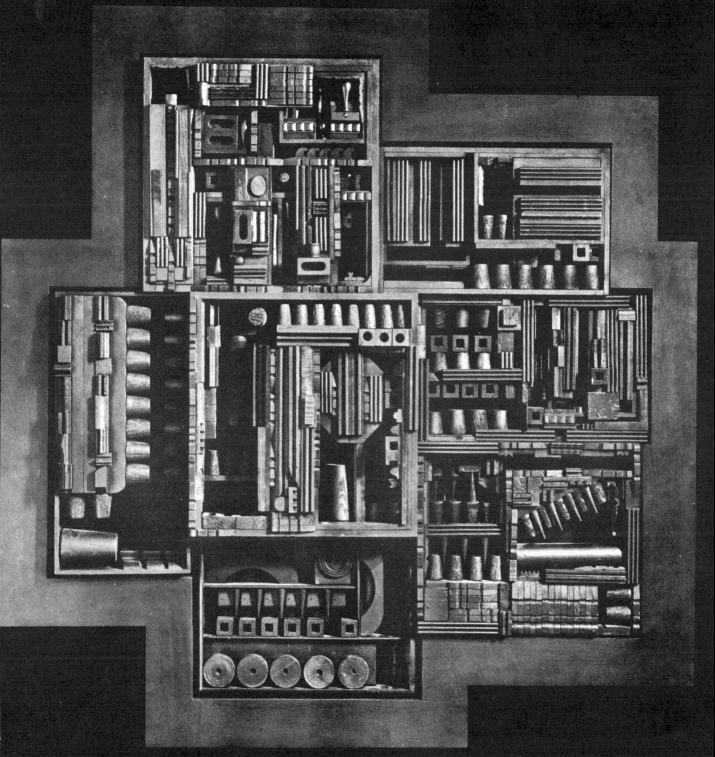

Quantum by Richard J. Chiara. A collage of license plates. The artist has taken a number of license plates of identical thickness and assembled them in vertical, horizontal, overlapping, and angular positions. A thick coating of paint has been applied to suggest that the composition has been intact for many years. A print probably could be made from this low-relief montage. (Reproduced by permission of the artist.)

Untitled. Assemblage of steel, canvas, cloth, and wire by Lee Bontecou (1960). This huge construction (5 by 6 feet) is 20 inches in depth. The form of the composition is made of steel; wire has been attached to vary its depth. Canvas and cloth of different colors and thicknesses were attached around the wire creating levels and openings of varying sizes. The surface of the assemblage resembles the terrain of the earth as seen from the air, and as the viewer walks around the construction, different impressions evolve. (Collection of Mr. and Mrs. Robert C. Scull, Great Neck, New York.)

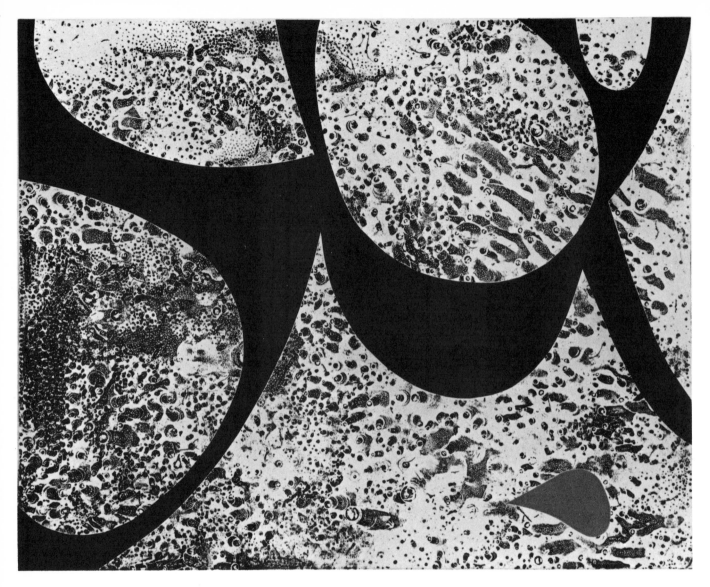

Hierophany by Myril Adler. The same
flat objects can be repositioned and inked
in varying colors to produce prints that
differ from each other but still possess
the identical overall elements.

Detail of *Altarpiece* by Norman Laliberté.

Collage Demonstrations with Printmaking Techniques

Collage and assemblage techniques are used with a high degree of imagination and skill by Myril Adler to create multicolored prints of great strength and sensitivity.

Mrs. Adler, whose watercolors, oils, and prints have been exhibited throughout the United States and in Europe, uses the collage concept in work that takes two different directions. Her prints are composed of segments and pieces of metal, wire, cardboard, screening and other low-relief objects, both found and manufactured, which are inked and run through an etching press to produce a print. This section will demonstrate the techniques she employs in creating her prints.

Once a print has been completed, Mrs. Adler will tear up or cut out of it certain graphic elements which become central themes in the creation of entirely new and individual works of art involving a multitude of materials including oil, acrylics, watercolor, Cellotex, insulation board, latex, and almost any useful material that comes to hand. In effect she creates (through the print medium) her own "found" objects that serve to stimulate and inspire the creation of entirely new compositions that have a mysterious and unique quality about them.

"My collages grow from different roots," Myril Adler says, "a personal vocabulary of texture and forms through the imprinting of rag papers with intaglio etching.

"I am stimulated by the brilliance of oil-based printer's inks which become fused with the paper through the great pressure of the etching press, and the endless variables of textured surface.

"In searching for an archetypal imagery I have evolved certain shapes, color combinations, and surfaces in which fragments taunt and intrigue me with their own possibilities. Torn, cut, painted into, pasted on flat, raised or carved surfaces, an endless variety of statements develop. In combination with dyes, inks, acrylic or oil paints the widest range of color hue and intensity becomes possible, from the pristine quality of the untreated paper to the deepest pool of multi-printed dark."

Though the print-making techniques outlined are important, what is significant to the student of collage, montage and assemblage is Mrs. Adler's creative use of self-made shapes and found objects and materials to produce prints that are imaginative compositions within themselves. At the same time, graphic elements within these prints are of such strength and stature that they can be torn or ripped from their original environment and used as "found" objects in the creation of new compositions.

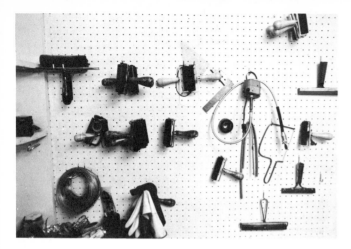

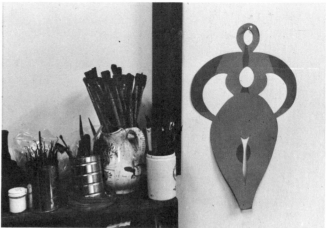

1. Some of the tools used in printmaking include rollers of varying size, hand drills, wire and metal instruments.

2. More working tools . . . brushes of different bristle quality, metal cutouts, shapes and forms, pins and nails.

3. The principal background of the composition is an intaglio zinc or copper plate that has been distressed and pockmarked by acid and with various power tools. Ink is being applied below the original level to cover the various surfaces and characteristics of the individual crevices and holes.

4. The excess ink — or ink that has remained on the flat plate surface — is cleaned off with a cloth.

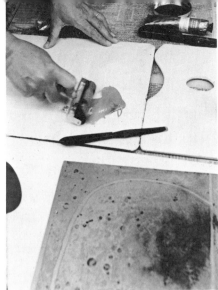

5. Many varieties of inks are used in a multitude of colors.

6. The ink is rolled back and forth on a paper before application to the plate in order to regulate its density and to assure that it will spread evenly.

7. The ink is applied to the surface of the plate. The holes and crevices were inked in a different color.

8. The form or shape — cut from a sheet of lithograph plating — is inked separately in its own color.

9. The wire — a found object in this case — is inked.

10. The two inked elements are positioned on the background intaglio plate.

137

11. The entire composition is now placed on the etching press.

12. A sheet of paper is placed over the composition. Experiments should be made with papers of different textures, qualities, and colors to produce prints that vary and have individual characteristics.

13. A blanket is placed over the paper before rolling the composition through the press.

14. Printing the composition.
The gauge of metal from which the figure was cut and the thickness of the wire (in addition to their individual color) leave an effective impression on the print, delineating and emphasizing elements within the composition; this could not be achieved if all the elements were done on a single surface plate. On the intaglio etching portion of the composition, the pressure of the press has fused the ink from the various surfaces with the paper to form an infinite variety of textures and rich, intense coloration.

1. A collection of hinges, lock and key hardware, metal and craft objects — some manufactured, others found — all of which can be used in collages for low-relief printmaking.

2 and 3. Selections of flat found and manufactured metal objects can be arranged in collage compositions and printed in one or more colors. As stated previously, papers of varying textures, weights, and colors should be tried out in making prints of this kind. Both hardware stores and junk shops contain a world of objects from which a variety of colorful, low-relief collage prints can be created.

Greek kylix, 6th century B.C. Vases and vessels of
this period were decorated with silhouette-like
figures and motifs illustrating events in everyday
life, fables and myths, and mourning scenes.
(Courtesy of The Montreal Museum of Fine Arts,
purchased 1939, gift of Harry A. Norton.)

SILHOUETTES, SHADOWS, AND CUTOUTS

Early History of the Silhouette

The silhouette is possibly the first art form known to man, its origins having been traced back some 20,000 to 30,000 years to Paleolithic or Stone Age peoples. The cave man (who probably never lived in dark, damp caves but, rather, in drier rock shelters) was preoccupied with hunting to obtain food in order to stay alive. Though primitive man lacked the skill to train animals for riding or to develop powerful weapons, he did have the facility to transmit graphically his beliefs, thoughts, dreams, superstitions, symbols, and premonitions as evidenced by silhouette-like drawings of animals and human figures found in limestone caves at Font-de-Gaume and Lascaux, France; in Altamira, Spain; at the Cape Colony of South Africa; in the Sahara Desert; in northern Australia and elsewhere.

No one is certain what these outline drawings of buffalo or bison, boars, foxes, wolves, deer, kangaroos, sprinting people and stencil-like renderings of the human hand were meant to represent, but it is thought that the truth may lie somewhere

between two theories projected by archaeologists and anthropologists. It has been suggested that the drawings (found in their most elaborate forms in the deepest recesses of the caves) were religious in concept. Others claim that the rough textures of the cave walls (many of the drawings have been found on rough rather than smooth surfaces) provoked a hallucinatory reaction in early man, which, much like modern "ink-blot" tests, triggered subconscious thoughts and emotions. Because food was foremost in the prehistoric mind, some anthropologists feel it is not unnatural for a subterranean contour to have suggested the arch of a meaty bison's back; thus it could have been that the cave artist completed the outline with charred bone or wood from his fire.

Many of these animals are drawn one over the other with spears and arrows protruding from each figure, suggesting that once the artist had gone through the ritual of "killing" his creation, the magical or divine forces attendant upon the images

he created would commit his vision to become a reality. Therefore, after the animal had been drawn (and "killed" pictorially), it was "dead" and could be drawn on top of or overlapped by the next picture without violating the artist's sense of visual reality.

It is difficult to make positive statements on the cave man's intent, but the artistic form of his expression—the silhouette or outline of the sharp shadow of an object—has prevailed since its humble beginning as the pioneer form of artistic expression, in which the vital forms of nature were committed to memory—and, in a broader sense, to history.

The silhouette is the foremost artistic device in the tomb and temple drawings and paintings of the Egyptian era of almost 6,000 years ago, when, rather than follow migrating beasts or journey in search of vegetation, man had learned to domesticate animals and to harvest by charting the changes of the seasons. The outline or silhouette drawing—with and without added embellishment—appeared in wall paintings, particularly in tombs, for the Egyptians believed that the spirit existed after life. If earthly possessions could not be buried with the body, at least they could be preserved in the tomb for spiritual use in the form of drawings, many of which were outlines or silhouettes.

This form of picture appears intermittently in Cretan art, from 2,500 to 1,000 B.C., on walls and pottery, and came to the fore with Greek civilization, beginning 1,000 B.C., and with the Etruscans. Silhouettes in the form of

figures or repetitive images or silhouette-like themes that resemble decorative patterns are most conspicuous on Greek pottery and ceramics used for conveying and storing water and wine. Unlike the cave men, who apparently drew to tempt magic spirits to smile favorably on their hunt, or the Egyptians, who created art to accompany the spirits of the dead, the Greeks painted scenes from life and their myths—events, feelings and emotions. Paintings on Greek pottery found today in museums around the world depict

mourning and funerary scenes, the feats of the gods and heroes (Hercules strangling a lion or feasting among the gods), javelin throwers, music lessons, bridal scenes—many of these expressed in silhouette form. More advanced and sophisticated concepts of representation using color, shading, tone, and the drawing of delicate detail were known then or were to follow. But in many instances, the silhouette took precedence because of its ability to communicate quickly on a basic level.

Ice Age paintings from the Agua Amarga caves in Spain. Silhouette paintings such as these depicting figures in flight (it is presumed that they were hunting animals or pursuing—or being pursued by—other peoples or fleeing the elements) have been found in many locations including South Africa and Scandinavia. (Reproduction by permission of © The New York Times Company and *Art In The Ice Age* by Maringer and Bandi, published by Frederick A. Praeger, Inc.)

Egyptian vase, circa 4000 B.C. Decorative and silhouetted motifs of this period eliminated overlapping and tended to simplify individual figures as well as to make full use of the elements of space and design. (Courtesy of The Montreal Museum of Fine Arts, purchased 1925, gift of Miss Mabel Molson.)

Opposite Page
Black-figured Panathenaic amphora. Greek, VI century B.C. The grace and spirit of the Greek athlete are captured in this remarkable silhouette painting. (Courtesy The Metropolitan Museum of Art, Rogers Fund, 1914.)

Queen Charlotte with her pet dog, a silhouette painted on glass by the English artist Jorden, now in the Royal Collection, Windsor Castle. It is believed that the silhouette form of illustration and portraiture stemmed from early attempts to trace the outline of the shadows of people and objects. Silhouette portraiture became truly popular in Europe during the Industrial Revolution with the ready availability of paper and cheaply priced scissors. (Photograph reproduced by gracious permission of Her Majesty Queen Elizabeth II.)

Silhouettes in the
17th, 18th, and 19th Centuries

The Greeks mastered the art of outlining the shadows of figures cast by sunlight and frequently completed their pictures by depicting the human face in silhouette form. Though these possessed the quality of identification (shadow figures of individuals prominent in Greek literature and drama have been preserved), they lacked personality and the effervescence of character.

Although silhouette and shadow or profile art existed in the Middle Ages, it did not gain in popularity because of superstition. In a number of beliefs and religions, the shadow was linked with the soul, and to draw it, walk across it, or allow one lower in society to cast his shadow upon you was to tamper with fate and invite disaster.

Long before the silhouette was commonly known it was referred to as "shadow" or "profile" art, "shades" or the "black" art. In portraiture it was executed by a number of methods. One of these was by seating the subject between a strong light and a waxed or oiled screen and having the artist blacken or paint in the shadow cast by the light. Frequently, projection equipment was used to reduce or enlarge the shadow cast, and, later, mechanical devices were invented which would enable the novice to execute faithfully shadow tracings and paint in or cut them out as the case may be.

As paper became readily available and with the development of cheaper scissors during the Industrial Revolution, still another method of silhouette making became popular: The artist merely cut the profile out of a piece of black paper. Many accomplished painters of the period did extremely fine work using this technique.

All these methods were prevalent during the Georgian period (1714-1813) in England, France, and Germany, but it was a Swiss patriot and author, Johann Caspar Lavatar, who gave the painted shadow of the profile prominence through the development of physiognomy, the "science" of judging characteristics and mental attitudes by observing facial features. Lavatar believed that character could be read by the profile, that the position of the lips, the chin, the eyebrows, the forehead, the slope and shape of the nose could reveal the character and personality of the individual and most times he used silhouettes as a means of explaining and practicing this theory.

In 1757, Etienne de Silhouette was named Finance Minister of France under Louis XV. De Silhouette planned drastic financial economies for the nation, patterned after those effectively used in England, and almost immediately became the laughing stock of the nation. His hobby was profile cutting, and unpopularity soon linked his name with this cheap form of portraiture in a derogatory sense. Within months, Etienne de Silhouette was out of office, but his name has remained as part of the language.

The profile painters of the 18th and early 19th century worked with cardboard and paper, glass, ivory, wax and plaster and many times introduced a color in addition to black or white, using crimson on black, a combination frequently seen in ancient Greek pottery. The age had many reputable artists, including John Field, who in the early 1800's made detailed silhouettes using gold embedded in glass, Anthing, a French portraitist who worked in Germany and England, Francois Torond, who specialized in the profile portrait and who openly advertised himself as a "Master of Drawing," August Edouart, one of the best-known and finest of paper cutters, Rosenberg, a refugee profile painter from Germany who became attached to the English Royal household, John Miers, who in the 1780's executed miniature profiles throughout Great Britain, A. Charles, who became known as a profilist of royalty, and Princess Elizabeth, daughter of George III, whose album of silhouettes has been preserved in the Royal Library at Windsor Castle.

Profile, shadow, and silhouette art flourished throughout Europe in many forms and distinctive characteristics. Its ready acceptance is attributed to general reaction against elaborately decorated and profusely ornamented architecture, interiors, furnishings and works of art of the late 17th and early 18th century. The silhouette form was adopted, too, by potters and textile makers who seemed to have journeyed back in time to the decorative style of the Greeks. An outstanding example of this were the profiled relief figures used by the Josiah Wedgwood potters.

"Hidden" silhouettes or profiles in art became popular during the French Revolution and the years that followed (1789 to 1848), providing a medium for the politically oppressed to express a clandestine or secret mode of hero worship.

Perhaps the best known American silhouette artist was William Henry Brown, who achieved fame by being able to cut remarkably realistic silhouettes—from memory if necessary—in but ten minutes.

In 1820, Louis J. M. Daguerre, a French painter, invented the daguerreotype, a means of photographing people and objects from a chemically treated metal or glass plate. Thirty years later, photography came into being. Like Etienne de Silhouette himself, the silhouette as an art form was soon retired from its prestigious position, and few recall the glory of its day.

Hidden silhouette of Napoleon. Hand-colored lithograph by Nathaniel Currier, circa 1835. The French Revolution produced this form of hidden subject material, which served to perpetuate the spirit and image of forbidden heroes for those politically oppressed. (Courtesy of The Metropolitan Museum of Art, New York, bequest of Mary Martin, 1938.)

A silhouette of Dixon Hall Lewis by one of the best known American silhouette artists, William Henry Brown, who worked many times from memory. A man of great charm, Brown was befriended by many prominent personalities. It took him just ten minutes to cut a silhouette for which he usually charged one dollar. (Courtesy of The Metropolitan Museum of Art, New York, bequest of Charles Allen Munn, 1924.

Detail from *Processional*,
pen and ink silhouette
by Norman Laliberté

Modern and Contemporary Silhouettes

The silhouette is no stranger to the 20th century for its appearance in the fields of advertising and communication, though many times unnoticed, is frequent. Its foremost attribute is to telegraph immediately a thought or idea in those areas of modern communications where speed is a prerequisite to understanding. Whether this is in the form of training pilots to recognize foreign aircraft against the horizon or to warn drivers that children are accustomed to crossing the road at a certain juncture, the silhouette does its job fully.

For many years psychologists have been making use of a free form of silhouette known as the Rorschach Test, wherein verbal response to what is suggested by a series of ink blots is used to determine unconscious thoughts and motivations. The silhouette has also been prevalent in education—in the teaching of elementary mathematics, for instance, where what is important to the learning process is instant recognition without cluttering or side-tracking the mind with detail unimportant to the correct answer.

The silhouette has become important, too, to children as a form of self-expression. Ask a child to decorate for Christmas or Hallowe'en and chances are that stars, trees, angels, cats, pumpkins and witches—silhouettes cut from solid colored paper—will emerge with little detail. Additional embellishment is unimportant or unnecessary for, to the child, these shapes alone amply symbolize the significance of the occasion.

In photography, the silhouette is frequently used to project a mood or an atmosphere. Thus it is that a silhouette-like photograph of baseball players limbering up in spring training projects the thought that the entire happening is much like a comical scene from a ballet. The silhouette succeeds in putting across not only the who? where? when? of the event, but a touch of the spirit of it, too.

In advertising and marketing the silhouette alone frequently communicates —almost in a flash, as it were—the image of a product, service or situation and, having achieved the impact of recognition, many times goes on to set the tone for the copy or sales pitch that is to follow. Television advertising and film trailers make good use of silhouettes. Within the limitations of the picture tube or screen such illustrations used with imagination are highly effective attention getters and, at the same time, project the spirit and quality of the commodity or program being advertised.

What is most apparent to those in communications and marketing is that the silhouette is international in character and significance. A tourist or traveller who does not speak the language of a strange country finds little difficulty in understanding that a cup and saucer silhouetted on a shop sign mean refreshments.

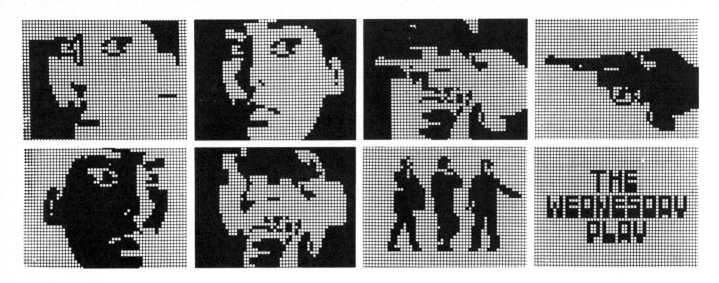

Trailer by Kenneth Brown for "The Wednesday Play." The graphic seems to grow visually as squares fill in (or, conversely, disappear) to form a picture in black or white. This electronic form of graphic art offers unlimited possibilities to the artist, and, because it provides the element of constant square-by-square growth, seems to fascinate the viewer more than the usual graphic. (Courtesy of the British Broadcasting Corporation, London.) *Left*. Detail.

Opposite Page
An ink drawing illustration by Milton Glaser, Push Pin Studios, New York. This sensitive silhouette depicts Capri, ". . . beautiful, horrible, haunted: that is the essence of what, about itself, Capri says to you . . ." The mechanically produced lined areas add an almost shimmering sense of relief to the foreboding spirit of the powerful black figures.

Right. Stills are photographed one at a time; in each frame the image has been placed slightly forward. A speeded-up projection of the strip gives the effect of movement. These multiple silhouette images were made in 1890 with a fixed plate camera.

Below. Early forerunner of a machine or projector that would eventually bring movement to still pictures. The black disc with slits was held before the eye. The disc with still pictures on it was placed immediately behind it. Both discs were whirled on the same axis. As the eye looked through the rotating slits, it caught glimpses of the rapidly rotating images on the second wheel, thus giving the illusion of a single figure in motion.

Opposite Page
This silhouette proves that perception depends on the eyes of the viewer. At first one sees the classic shape of a goblet, but, upon closer scrutiny, the object disappears and the background takes over, revealing two profiles. (Reproduced with special permission of John Wiley and Sons, Inc., New York.

Decorative cutouts are affixed to an egg.

The Shadow Play

The Egyptians of the 11th to 13th century were known to have cut ornamental silhouettes out of leather and vellum, reminiscent of the figures used in shadow plays. However, this form of art or entertainment is said to have originated in China, from whence it spread to India, Java, Persia, Turkey, Greece, the Moslem countries of North Africa, and, by the 17th and 18th centuries, to Europe.

The Chinese originally used a hollow ball, the outside of which was perforated with minute and intricate patterns. A lighted candle was ingeniously set inside the ball so that when the ball was manipulated or rolled, the candle remained upright and projected shadow patterns on a screen or wall. Later, the Chinese developed shadow plays with puppet figures made of donkey hide dyed in bright colors, which were projected on a screen.

An early 19th-century Japanese perforated silver globe with built-in gimbals for the support of an inside fixture. A lighted candle is inserted and ingeniously remains upright as the ball is rolled, throwing reflections of the perforations and the delicate filigree patterns on the wall. Such devices, originating in the Orient, were forerunners of shadow plays and theatres. (Courtesy the Royal Ontario Museum, University of Toronto.)

Shadow plays, which concerned themselves with religious and legendary topics, are thought to have their roots in the Han Dynasty.

Shadow plays were exceedingly popular in Java and were performed on all national and ceremonial occasions. Their puppets were made of buffalo skin and manipulated by rods.

In Turkey, the principal and most popular puppet characters (made of highly colored camel skin) were known as Karagöz and Hadijivad, who frequently performed vulgar comic routines and vignettes. These same puppet characters later dominated the shadow plays of the North Africans and provided the slapstick and ridicule elements in some of the plays that were to come to Europe.

Italy was probably the first European nation to popularize the shadow play, for the idea took root there as early as the 17th century. In the 18th century the "Ombres Chinoises" (lacking the Chinese color projection, for most European shadow plays were in black) came to Versailles. Before long the shadow theatre graduated from a street corner show to sophisticated café and cabaret entertainment which featured especially written plays on contemporary topics.

Shadow plays were popular in England, Switzerland, and Germany as well as in the United States in the 18th century. In 1893, shadow plays such as those performed in the night clubs of Paris were featured at the Chicago World's Fair, but these performances proved more of a curiosity than a stimulation to the development of the art. A more exciting medium was in the offing—the motion picture.

Poster by Milton Glaser announcing an unusual theatrical entertainment The exuberant figures are silhouetted in graduated color tones against a black background.

A mid-19th-century Chinese shadow puppet made of hide and painted in color. The shadow play is thought to have its roots in the Han Dynasty. Chinese shadow plays stressed religious and legendary tnemes. (Courtesy the Cooper Union for the Advancement of Science and Art, New York.)

Shadow puppets for "Le Ballet de Cendrillon" from the Théâtre Séraphin in the Palais Royal, Paris, which was popular from the late 18th to the mid 19th century. Sophisticated shadow theatre became the vogue, and plays—many of a satirical political nature—were especially written for them. (Courtesy of the Cooper Union for the Advancement of Science and Art, New York.)

Cutouts

Decorative cutout work has existed as a widespread art activity for thousands of years. The oldest known examples go back to the Egyptians of 1400 B.C.

In the 18th century, highly artistic cutouts were made by German nuns. But the most elaborate, intricate, and imaginative originated in, and are still coming from, small Polish rural communities, where cut-work has become an integral part of folk cultural expression. Here, paper cutting appears to be an extension of an ancient custom of cutting figures and motifs from cloth, leather, or tree bark and affixing them, in a decorative sense, to clothing, walls, and pieces of furniture in the home. While silhouette cutting prospered in Europe,

the Polish peasants, influenced by symbols and designs from their religion and lore, turned their intuitive talents towards creating out of paper the "wycinanki"—beautiful designs, patterns, and stylized figures and symbols which reflect aspects of their culture and beliefs.

The Polish folk art is created by use of ordinary knives or thick sheep-shearing scissors. The paper is folded, manipulated, and twisted during the completely spontaneous cutout process (Polish cutouts are never predrawn). Frequently, a wycinanki of one color is superimposed over another of a different color, in order to build up or elaborate on a design.

The overall patterns are geometric and sometimes kaleidoscopic in effect, perhaps

owing their origin to motifs stemming from the ancient peoples of Northern Europe—interlaced circles, rectangles, squares and markings that were believed to have magical powers. Other significant influences in the design of an individual wycinanki are religion (it is thought that they were first popularized among folk people as a home decoration at Easter), folklore, and happenings that highlight life in the forest or on the farm.

Children everywhere enjoy cutting paper objects with scissors, particularly in decorating homes or school rooms on festive occasions. Skillful use of scissors and paper has also given competent artists still another means of achieving highly sophisticated shapes and figures.

Opposite page

Polish "wycinanki" cutouts made by village folk. Guided by an almost instinctive decorative sense, young people, who frequently lack any skill at drawing, execute complicated designs using crude knives or shears. Many of the symbols that emerge in the patterns are traditional, originating in religion and folklore. (Photographs courtesy of Shirley Glaser.)

Blue Nude with Flowing Hair by Henri
Matisse, a cut gouache 42½ by 32½ inches.
Matisse first made paper cutouts in 1931,
when he was 62, as a means of experimenting
in design with movable shapes and forms.
In *Last Works of Henri Matisse* by Monroe
Wheeler, published by The Museum of
Modern Art, New York, he is quoted as
saying that he believed in indefatigable
preparation and experiment—to arrive at
simplicity and forthrightness in the end.
Matisse worked in cut-and-pasted gouache
compositions from the early '50's until his
death in 1954. *Blue Nude with Flowing Hair*
depicted here is one of a series which he
began experimenting with in 1952, some of
which were later to appear in one of his
major murals. (Courtesy of private
collection, Paris.)

Opposite Page
A cutout by Richie Kehl. The razor blade is
used free hand, as if it were a drawing
pencil. The composition is quickly slashed out
and mounted on a black background. The
overall outline is, therefore, born of
complete spontaneity.

Detail from *The Kill of the Bison*, brush and ink silhouette by Norman Laliberté.

Projects in Silhouettes and Cutouts

There are any number of cutout and silhouette projects which can be carried out easily with readily available materials. These include the intricate steps of Polish wyci nanki cutting, decorating rocks, eggs, and other surfaces with cutouts and silhouette-like patterns, ripout compositions, children's cutouts at holiday and festival time, and mural making with cutout and silhouette shapes.

The cutout is one of the first art techniques made available to children. Most kindergartens and nurseries provide blunt scissors and colored construction paper almost from their pupils' first day in class. Scissors and pride of creativity are synonymous. The finished cutout

may not look anything like the witch the child intended to shape, but to him it looks like a witch and he is proud of if. At that precise moment of his development, it is as artistic and as creative as any work he may have produced with crayons or paint brush.

Projects involving cutouts and silhouettes present a unique challenge to the serious young art student—an opportunity to experiment with space and composition and to discover the artistic potential of contrasts, reverse images, and the juxtaposition of solid cutouts of varying shapes, textures, weights, and dimensions.

Most times, cutouts and silhouettes involve virtually no preplanning or predetermined sketches, and perhaps this represents their greatest fascination and potential. The real challenge is to draw upon and to accelerate the development of the student's intuitive sense of creativity and design and to blend these elements with the mood of the moment and the spirit of the environment in which he is working. The result is the mustering of a creative spontaneity and the experience of having produced a work that is individually unique, highly imaginative, graphically stimulating, and of immense personal satisfaction.

Opposite Page

A montage of silhouettes and cutouts employing varied techniques and combinations: cutouts and inks, cutouts and pen drawing of detail, brushed ink drawings, large area cutouts with details added in ink, pasted shapes used experimentally, paper ripouts with felt-nib pen details, multiple uses of cutouts in combination with other materials, negative cutouts with pen-and-ink detail inserts, and the overlapping of black on black to attain tone and textures.

Examples of cutouts with added images from various sources, including graphic elements from magazines and newspapers. These cutouts commenced with the image or figure from the magazine and were developed from that point with the use of black paper cut out with pinking shears. Some are part silhouettes, part drawing, a melange of forms and shapes.

Page 168

The American Dream by Norman Laliberté. The jagged line of the pinking shears adds to the waving of the stripes and gives an optical effect.

Page 169

Dream by Norman Laliberté. An illustrative page for a legend, formed with a collage of found and made images which produce a poetic feeling.

WOODCUTS

Early History of Woodcuts

The history of the woodcut is a fascinating chapter in the evolution of man's ability to communicate through an art medium.

The woodcut originated in the Far East where, over two thousand years ago, carved or engraved wooden blocks were used to make symbolic, decorative, and religious design impressions on clay or wax surfaces.

By the second century A.D., the Chinese were wood block printing on paper, a technique which was soon to be introduced in Japan as a religious art form. Though the Phoenicians were known to have brought Indian wood block printed fabrics westward before the time of Alexander the Great, woodcut printing developed in Europe only as paper became readily available.

In the eleventh century, with the import of paper from the Far East, some woodcut printing took place in Spain. However, it was not until paper began to be manufactured in Germany and France at the turn of the fourteenth century that the medium truly took hold on the Continent. The first known woodcut — depicting Buddha in a Chinese manuscript — is said to have been executed in A.D. 868, but among the earliest examples known today are a *Madonna with Four Virgin Saints in a Garden*, believed to have been carved in 1418 (Bibliothèque Royale, Brussels), and a German *St. Christopher*, pulled in the year 1423 (John Rylands Library, Manchester). The woodcut, particularly renditions of Biblical themes, flourished in both France and Germany during this period. These prints were soon prevalent in Austria, Bohemia, Bavaria, and other areas of Europe.

By the mid-fifteenth century, crude but usable playing cards were being produced with the woodcut technique. But this era heralded a development of greater significance: the invention of movable type. At this time, entire pages of books — illustrations as well as text — were carved and reproduced through the woodcut method. Known as "block-book" printing, the technique is believed to have originated in the Netherlands in 1470; it was still in practice in Rome in 1548. Whether or not the painstaking block-book carving of text stimulated the invention of movable type (which, of course, was reusable) has been debated. What cannot be denied is that block-book printing thrived during the period: beautifully illustrated religious volumes produced in Florence and Venice testify to this.

By the sixteenth century the popularity of the woodcut had reached full fruition through the work of Albrecht Dürer. Born in Nuremberg in 1471. Dürer was apprenticed for three years to the painter Michael Wolgemut, whose workshop produced many of the woodcut illustrations for books of that time.

Dürer's contribution to the medium was both prolific and dynamic: not only did he encourage other artists throughout Europe toward perfecting the technique, but his influence was felt in the adaptation of subject matter other than religion, including politics, comment on social movements of the time, caricature, cartooning, and criticism.

Under patronage of Emperor Maximilian, many ambitious book illustration projects were initiated. Thus encouraged, Dürer and others (including Hans Holbein the Younger and Lucas van Leyden in Germany and Campagnola and de' Barbari in Italy) continued their efforts in developing the woodcut toward a medium of mass appeal and acceptance.

Dürer died in the year 1528. Two decades later, with the advent of line engraving and etching reproduction, the popularity of the woodcut medium declined sharply. Some 200 years were to pass before it would flourish again.

Detail of a woodcut from 1756 that served as a business card for a pin manufacturing company.

Woodcut astrological figures by Leopold of Austria from *De Astrorum Scientia*, published in Augsburg, 1489. (Reproduced courtesy Victoria and Albert Museum London.)

♒ **Aquarius**   ♓ **Pisces**   ♈ **Aries**   ♉ **Thaurus**

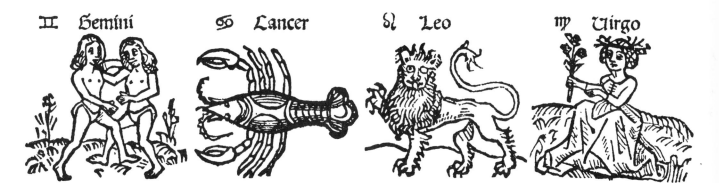

♊ **Gemini**   ♋ **Cancer**   ♌ **Leo**   ♍ **Virgo**

♎ **Libra**   ♏ **Scorpius**   ♐ **Sagittarius**   ♑ **Capricornus**

Opposite Page
The Kiss by Edvard Munch. A single form almost devoid of hands or arms has created a man and woman in emotional embrace. The starkness of the black figures is contrasted against the natural, overwhelming grain of the background and adds a strong sense of drama to the composition. (Reproduced courtesy Oslo Kommunes Kunstamlinger Munch Museet, Norway.)

Detail from woodcut by Norman Laliberté.

Master and Contemporary Woodcuts

Thomas Bewick, whose beautiful white-line illustrations of the world of nature revived woodcut and wood engraving printing, was a great influence on the artists of his era. In England, William Blake and others were to follow in this technique; in France, a new age of wood engraving came into being with the romantic volume or book, richly illustrated by artists such as Doré, Johannt, Gavarni, Monnier, and Meissonier.

Important to the development of the woodcut as a modern art influence is the prolific work of Katsushika Hokusai. In his lifetime (1760-1849), this great Japanese artist produced some 30,000 compositions — a good many of them under pseudonyms, a Japanese practice of the time.

During his 90 years of life, Hokusai — through single and multi-colored woodcuts and wood engravings —

depicted many aspects of Japan: its natural beauty, the good or rigorous life of its people, their religious and philosophical beliefs. As an illustrator of both literature and life, he was known to be restless, dissatisfied, and (as he once wrote) seeking the time when ". . . every line and dot I draw will be imbued with life . . ." Hokusai gave the woodcut and wood block print scope and flexibility. His compositions have served for students in all media as virtual manuals in the study of purity and forcefulness of line, rhythm, and the use of space.

By the mid-eighteenth century, the black-line method of woodcut illustration was being popularized in England by the Dalziel brothers; but, with the rapid development of photo-mechanical means of reproduction, this revival was short-lived. Simultaneous with developments in

America, the English woodcut was moving from a medium used basically for illustration to an independent form of artistic expression.

Perhaps the first artist of major importance to steer it in this direction was Paul Gauguin; in 1894 Gauguin returned to France from his Tahitian adventure with ten wood block two-tone color compositions. Though the techniques Gauguin used for this work were interesting and complex, of greater importance is the impetus he gave the medium by initiating an awareness of its full potentialities. Other great artists in Europe, America, and the Far East were to explore further and find permanent expression through the woodcut and wood engraving. These included Edvard Munch, who was able to derive a forceful and haunting style through the nature of the wood itself; Ernst Ludwig Kirchner, Emil Nolde,

Christian Rohlfs, and others of this era. They explored the basic essentials of wood, producing prints of great strength or sensitivity, as the case might be, but always of vitality.

During the 1920s and 1930s the woodcut and wood engraving medium was kept vigorous in the United States by artists such as Rockwell Kent, Eric Gill, and Thomas Nason. In Japan, Shiko Munakata's powerful wood block prints, influenced by the folklore and Buddhist belief of his people, began to emerge; by mid-century, they were to achieve a unique position of universal artistic influence. By the mid '40s and early '50s, Misch Kohn, Antonio Frasconi, Leonard Baskin, and other artists in America were giving the woodcut and wood engraving new direction and impetus, which have influenced seriously still other young artists in the medium.

This section indicates something of the success of twentieth-century artists in the medium and discusses some of the techniques they have employed. Because of space limitations, it is not possible to depict the interesting and notable compositions of many others working in this field today. Still, the following pages represent a worthy cross-section of an art form which again pulsates with challenge and potentiality.

Opposite Page

Zuerichsee by Ernst Ludwig Kirchner (1880-1938. There is a great deal of activity reflected in the woodcut by Kirchner, a leader of the Expressionist movement of his day. One sees boats, a steamship, fishermen, canoes and rowboats. The water is alive and all the action appears to be coming toward the viewer. The procession of people going back and forth across the bridge increases the action.

Above, left. Self-portrait by Käthe Kollwitz, 1923. *Above, right.* Selbstildnis (self-portrait) by Max Beckmann, 1922. *Below, left. Hugo Biallowons* by Ernst Ludwig Kirchner, 1916. *Below, right. Baertiger Mann* by Erich Heckel, 1908. It is interesting to compare the composition techniques employed by these foremost German woodcut artists. Beckmann has isolated the face in order to give it strength, while the Kollwitz face is buried in the black so that it appears to emerge from and yet, at the same time, be swallowed by it. Kirchner has used black to give the face greater drama; Heckel, on the contrary, achieves his dramatic effect by using a great deal of white in his composition. The irregular lettering in the Kirchner woodcut appears to be a product of the woodcutting process and readily becomes a part of the overall design.

Das Tor, 1920, a woodcut by Lionel Feininger. Despite the fact that this composition is predominantly white, it conveys a strong visual impact.

Opposite Page

Woodcut by Misch Kohn. The artist has given deliberate thought to the placement and execution of each line and every dot. Each black and white area plays against the others, and the overall effect is a fully planned composition.

178

The '30s, an illustration by Seymour Chwast for *Push Pin Graphics, No. 36*. An elegant board meeting in a hotel suite. The stark figures are crowded into the center of the work, while at its extremities abstract patterns of ferns and mosaic flooring arrest the viewer's attention. The table of Eastern design serves as a visual break between the hulking figures and the fine details at the room's perimeter. (Reproduced courtesy Push Pin Studios, Inc., New York.)

182

Wood-type composite collage by Murray Tinkelman. The artist has used actual wood block type faces — most of them carved by hand from hard cherry wood — to form an assemblage of letters. These were glued onto a piece of plywood which was then cut into a circle four feet in diameter. A print could be pulled from this low relief, mammoth woodcut of letters.

Detail from woodcut by Norman Laliberté.

Woodcut Demonstration and Projects

This chapter provides step-by-step procedures and techniques for carrying out a number of woodcut print projects.

The traditional form of carving a woodcut and printing from it is demonstrated by artist Bill Greer, who uses two squares of pine to produce a floral composition of appeal and sensitivity.

Norman Laliberté demonstrates a number of woodcut techniques working in pine, Masonite, and plywood, illustrating both flexibility in the use of wood and paper materials and spontaneity in working with manual and power tools.

A number of points should be kept in mind when carrying out projects such as these:

Preliminary drawings: these should be sketchy; their purpose should be to provide guidance and general definition to the drawing rather than exact cutting lines. (In the traditional woodcut procedure, as demonstrated by Bill Greer, detailed drawing *is* necessary.)

Tools: these should be used with dexterity and a spirit of freedom. Safety, however, should always be a key factor. Use bits and cutting instruments as you would a pencil. Remember that cutting tools or rotary bits have different impressions. Be selective according to the line required.

Paper: experiment! Use a variety of papers in an array of colors; different weights and textures of paper yield interesting results.

Inks: remember that there are a multitude of printing inks in addition to black.

Wood: use the other side of your pine block and relate it to your original composition. Pick interesting shapes and pieces off the workshop floor; these present unusual hand-stamping potential.

The finished print: this need not be the end, but rather the beginning. Multiple image and overlapping can add vitality to a print. Graphic elements within a print can be cut or torn from their environment and reassembled elsewhere to form the basis of a new work of art, to be enlarged or embellished in other media. Intact, any print can be given effervescence and enlargement by continuing to work on it with pastels, oil crayons, color pencils, chalks and dyes. Papers colored with pastels or other media before they are applied to the ink block yield interesting and unusual effects. A finished print, while still wet, can be sprinkled with metallic powder to completely transform the composition and bring it new brilliance. In essence, the print need not be the end, but rather — with experimentation — it can be the beginning and inspiration for a unique and highly individual work of art.

A number of finished compositions by Norman Laliberté, on paper, cloth, and fabric produced from pine, Masonite and plywood, complete the chapter.

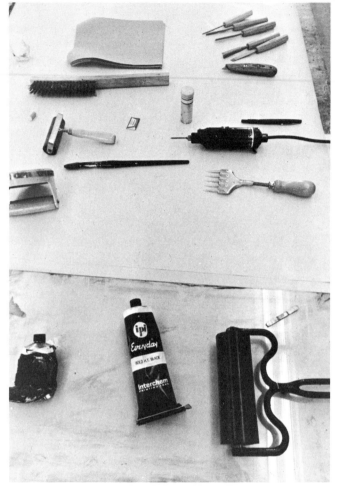

1. and 2.   Photographed are the various tools and materials used in this woodcut demonstration by artist Bill Greer. Included are nails of varying sizes and thicknesses, hard wire brushes, an ice pick, razor blades, various mechanical and woodcutting hand tools, rollers, and a selection of papers of different quality, weight, color and texture.

All photographs in this section are by Richard Braaten.

3. The artist makes his preliminary sketch or drawing on a piece of paper.

4. The boards for a diptych (two piece) composition are cut from a piece of pine. The boards are clear-grained and without knots.

5. The drawing is made directly on the board with a Pentel pen. A brush and ink can also be used for this purpose. The blacked in or drawn areas will remain uncut and therefore will reproduce when inked.

6. Another method of delineating the drawing is to paint the entire surface of the block with black ink. When dry, the design or composition is drawn over the black with chalk. This gives the artist a better idea of the character of the finished woodcut, since in this method the white or chalked areas are cut away. Cutting is done in the direction away from the artist and against a stationery piece of wood which absorbs the motion of the cut while keeping the woodcut block in place.

7. Cutting out larger sections of the wood.

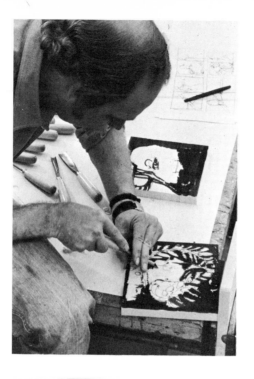

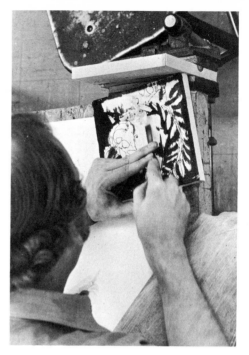

8. Cutting is done along the grain of the wood. If the composition has a border, care must be taken to arrest the pressure of the cut before the edge hits the area to remain intact.

9. Bill Greer varies the tools in accordance with the nature of the cut that is required: coarse instruments are available for gouging large areas of wood; very fine tools are used for cutting more intricate details. Pine is a soft wood, and therefore, all tools must be sharp.

186

10, 11, 12.
The tools used vary in accordance with the character of the detail being cut. For instance, a very fine instrument is used to delineate the stem of a flower, while a broader knife gives definition to the nature or substance of a leaf. In itself, the block is a composition of beauty with its carving and hollows of varying depth and the imprint of the different tools. Much of this beauty, of course, will not register on the print because it exists below the printing surface. Fine detail in the composition is added with nail point and razor blade scratching and etching.

13. The blocks are inked with a roller.

14. Paper is placed over the blocks and rubbed with a clean roller.

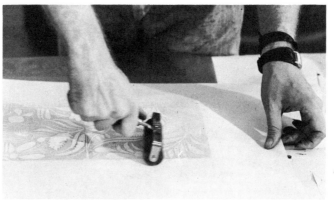

15. The paper may also be rubbed by hand with a cloth.

16.   The woodcut print is pulled from the blocks.

17.   The carved wood blocks and the print which they produced.

The blocks can be printed in almost any color on different kinds and weights of paper as well as on unusually textured and colored paper stocks. Interesting prints can also be made on fabrics and cloth. Multiple images, over-prints and double exposures are all possible because the blocks can be inked and handled with comparative ease.

This doll print was produced in the hand stamping technique. A rough outline of a doll was first sketched in negative with brushed ink on a 3 inch plank. The band was then used almost as a drawing instrument to determine the exact outline of the doll. Decorative and feature details were cut into the surface by using a variety of rotary bits almost as if they were pencils of various sizes and densities. Cross-hatch strokes were cut into the background areas which could not be cut away and therefore would reproduce in the print, while deep-cutting bits eliminated areas not to appear in the printed compositions. Fine detail was added with sharp nail scratching. The surface was brushed and sandpapered, then inked. Printing and hand-stamping were made on papers of varying weights, colors and textures.

A Masonite woodcut by Norman Laliberté. The basic form was cut with the use of a power saw. Details were scratched or incised into the form by a power tool. Additional scratches were applied by hand with a sharp nail. The form was inked with a printer's roller.

THE ART OF STENCIL

Early History of the Stencil

The stencil is one of the earliest decorative forms known to man. It was used by the Egyptians of the pyramid era, by the Chinese at the time they built the Great Wall, and by both primitive and civilized people throughout the world in almost every historic age which required decorative patterns and images on a repeat or multiple basis.

The basic stencil process has remained the same throughout the ages. An open image, design or pattern is drawn onto and then cut out of an impervious piece of material. The material (which is now a stencil) is pressed or held flat against the object to be decorated, and color in the form of paint, crayon (or whatever medium is being used) is applied by brushing, dabbing or filling in the open or cut-out areas of the stencil. This open stencil method was common to early civilizations in decorating interior and exterior walls, furnishings, fabrics, wares, and utensils.

Stencilling has been a decorative technique of primitive peoples in many places, including the South Pacific and North and Central America, and is believed to have predated by many centuries the European influence in

these areas. Applications of stencil designs are evident on many pieces of American Indian ceramics dating back to prehistoric times. The first explorers of the Fiji Islands were surprised to see beautiful geometric designs printed onto coarse bark cloth by means of stencils cut out of banana leaves.

There are many early evidences of the use of stencils among so-called civilized people. It is known that the stencil was used by early Greek and Etruscan civilizations and that Buddhist artists of several thousand years ago decorated early temples and monasteries by means of stencil art.

There are many instances of the use of stencil in producing religious manuscripts dating from the period 600-800 A.D. At that time it was used not only as a means of producing a repetitive, decorative element but of duplicating words as well as a primitive form of printing. Authentic examples of Japanese cloth decorated with designs applied by the stencil process go back to the year 710 A.D. The stencil has been an integral element in Japanese folk art and textile printing throughout the known history of that nation.

The introduction of paper into Europe brought with it many opportunities for stencilling, which already was popular as a decorative art in many countries on that continent prior to the Middle Ages. Embroidery and tapestry, carving in wood, glass, precious metals, and ivory — produced by means of the stencil process — were quite common in cathedrals and wealthy manors of the time. Many people of lesser means used the stencil also to apply decorative touches to and beautify walls, floors, and furniture.

There is a close alliance between the early European use of stencils and the development of printing with wood blocks and then with movable type. The earliest playing cards we know — dating from the year 1440 — are believed by some to have been produced by means of stencil. The playing cards which followed — and to an extent manuscripts, decorative sheets, and religious renderings — were printed by woodcut and wood block, then hand-colored by stencil application of paint or ink. Printing and stencil decorating (or "enlivening," as it was sometimes called) worked hand in hand in this manner in many instances from the 15th to 19th century.

In the 17th century the stencil played a major part in the development of the wallpaper industry. Pioneered by Jean Papillon of France, matching wallpaper sheets known as "domino" papers were colored and printed by stencil and became popular throughout Europe. The stencil also became available for decorating individual pieces of furniture, panels, and repeat borders on walls and floors. Its popularity as a decorative art form was immediately prevalent in early America and was common in homes throughout Massachusetts, Connecticut, Rhode Island, Vermont, New York, New Hampshire, Ohio, and Maine as far back as the late 1700s. The United Empire Loyalists fleeing north from this area during the American Revolution (1776-1787) brought some aspects of stencil art to their new homes in Upper and Lower Canada and the Atlantic Provinces.

It has been maintained that some of the more similar cave drawings dating back tens of thousands of years may have been produced by means of a primitive stencil or form-tracing process of one kind or another. Though the creating of a stencil itself requires the skill of an artist or craftsman, stencil application in most cases is a simple process within the range of most people's ability. This ready accessibility to almost everyone, along with the practicality of immediate result, has been responsible for the great popularity and personal charm of the stencil as a decorative art and a recreational activity for hundreds of years.

In this Victorian stencil the heaviness of the dark lines and the lightness of the curved scroll and circle forms tend to compete with each other to produce a well-balanced and pleasing design.

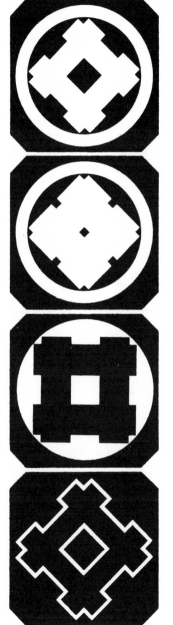

A series of Japanese family crests. These seem to be similarly shaped in tic-tac-toe style, yet each crest is entirely different from the others. Some of the designs are open, others criss-cross, still others are closed, filled in or varied with round edges or square corners. Japanese stencil designs, such as these, many times were based on religious or mythological concepts.

A Japanese stencil-letter written during the mid-nineteenth century. Though these letter forms are old, their flow and placement have something of a contemporary sophistication about them.

195

Music Box. Wood, glass, and metal construction by Robert Rauschenberg (1951). The combination of a found crate, coarse wood, and nails which seems to match the character of the stencilled letters makes this a most interesting construction with almost medieval overtones. (Reproduced courtesy Dayton's Gallery 12, Minneapolis.)

Spirograph drawing. The Spirograph is a form of plastic stencil which, in a way, is a continuation of the player-piano principle (which produced sound) and the teletypesetter concept (which results in manufactured print). By varying the holes used in the Spirograph, designs of an elegant and lyrical quality can be drawn. Also see pages 202 and 203.

Modern and Contemporary Stencils

During the Renaissance, artists used the technique of stencil "pouncing" to transfer the outlines of preliminary drawings to walls and panel surfaces for compositions to be completed in tempera and other media. The method was simple and effective: a series of holes was punched into a large sheet of paper outlining the contour line of a drawn composition. The paper was then held against the surface of the wall or panel, and dusting powder or powdered charcoal was pounced over the holes. After the paper was removed, the dotted outline or form of the work appeared on the area to be painted. It was a convenient way of assuring proper proportions and guidelines for major paintings often being executed in difficult working areas such as ceilings and high walls.

But stencil images, forms, and letters did not appear in the compositions of fine artists until the early 1900s, when Braque and Picasso pioneered the collage medium. Commenting on this new practice, the French *avant-garde* poet and writer, Guillaume Apollinaire wrote ". . . it is perfectly legitimate to use numbers and printed letters as pictorial elements; new in art, they are already soaked with humanity." As artists experimented with pasting letters, numerals, symbols, and images onto their work, it is understandable that graphic elements applied through stencil outline tracings soon would be included as vital facets of composition expression.

There are many contemporary artists working with stencils in a wide variety of techniques; this chapter illustrates some of the variations they employ. The silk-screen work of Andy Warhol is depicted through the now familiar soup carton and the multiple-image impact of the human form and face. The stencil has been an integral ingredient in compositions by Jasper Johns, whose still-life presentations of objects and images reflect the tense complexities of the frightening technological age that is upon us. In the composition *Don't Fall and Me*, Larry Rivers not only creates forms and images by means of stencil, but includes an actual stencil as part of his collage-composition.

Robert Rauschenberg creates a foreboding, medieval construction from a found crate, a fusillade of nails, and stencil letters which take on the coarse, cross-cut texture of the wood. These are but a few of the examples reproduced here.

Unlike stencilled folk art, which finds beauty of a kind by means of placement and repetition, the contemporary artist appears to begin his stencil techniques at these former points of limitation and works in every conceivable and inconceivable direction. The stencil may provide rigid borders or perimeters with respect to form and space, but technique, method, and form of application are curtailed only by the extent of individual creativity.

Above. Detail from *Ten Numbers*. Pencil on paper by Jasper Johns (1960). (Collection of Ted Carey. Reproduced courtesy of Leo Castelli Gallery, New York. Photo by Rudolph Buckhardt.)

Below. *Don't Fall and Me*. Oil and collage on canvas mounted on wood by Larry Rivers (1966). (Reproduced courtesy of John H. Moore and the Marlborough-Gerson Gallery, Inc., New York. Photo by Nathan Rabin.)

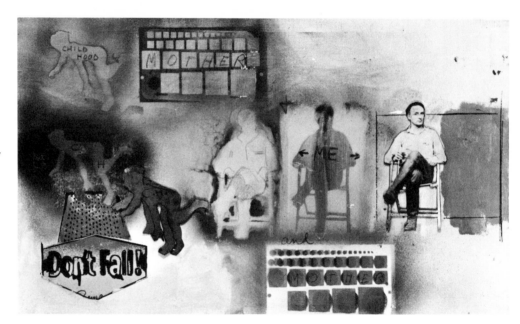

Opposite Page

Parts of the Face—French Vocabulary Lesson, 1961, oil on canvas by Larry Rivers. The head has been painted loosely and is somewhat incomplete, while the stencilled words leading to the parts of the face are deliberate and positioned in a most accurate manner. (Reproduced courtesy of the Tate Gallery, London.)

CHEVEUX

FRONT

SOURCIL

CIL

OEIL

JOUE

NEZ

DENT

LÈVRE

MENTON

199

Jackie, 1964, acrylic and enamel silk-screened on canvas by Andy Warhol. Instead of isolating one object, the artist has taken a silk-screen stencil and printed it in a series of multiples. The sheer repetition of the same image gives the composition strength and a sense of drama. The background of each image varies in color; this is an conomical way of providing tone, mood, and emphasis to a multiple image of this category. (From the Stroher Collection. Reproduced courtesy Ace-Canada-Ltd., Vancouver. Photo by Rudolph Burckhardt.)

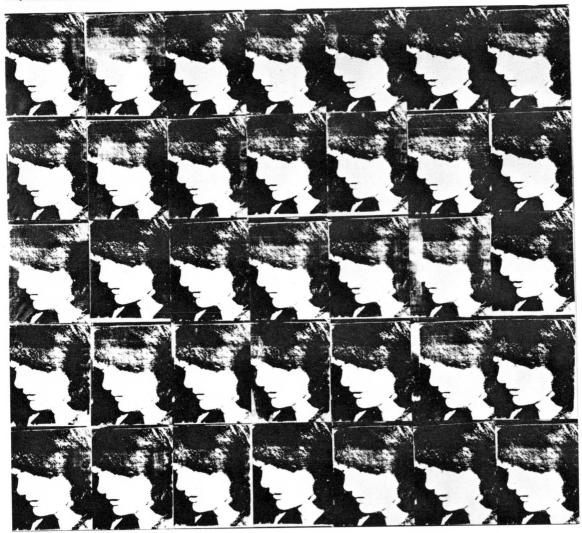

Opposite Page

The Calumet, 1961, oil on canvas by Robert Indiana. The artist has created a series of circles and stars of varying sizes and added stencilled letters to unite them as a composition. The words are as clear as labels and extremely legible so that a verbal-visual image is immediately apparent. This kind of stencil lettering is almost the only type face that can be used to convey the information projected through a composition of this quality. (Reproduced courtesy Brandeis University. Photo by John D. Schiff.)

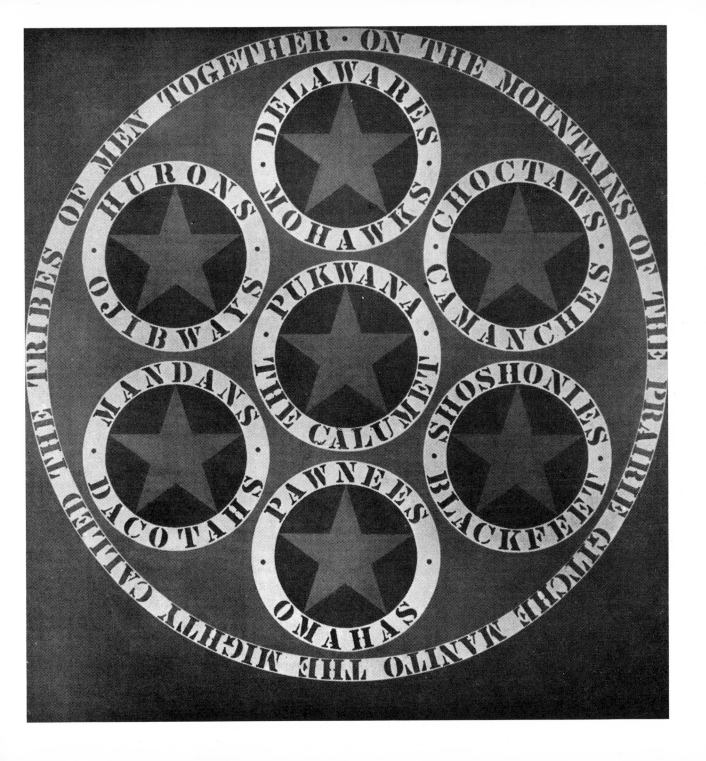

Rhythmic line drawing made with a Spirograph stencil.

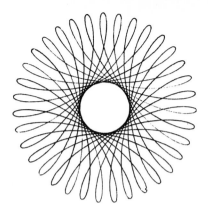

Stencil Projects

An almost limitless number of projects can be done by the stencil process. This chapter outlines some of them and concludes with Norman Laliberté's stencil compositions, which often have resulted not from preconceived intention but rather from experimentation while in the process of execution. It is this spirit of exploration on the part of the artist that is paramount to the success of these projects and to the use of the stencil in a serious composition.

Several stencil techniques are demonstrated through the following projects which have been devised by Laliberté, including multiple image, overlapping, off-register, reversing, flopping, printing from the back or reverse side of the stencil after it has been used initially, overprinting, positive and negative forms, using the stencil itself within the composition, stencilling from assembled strips and pieces of paper, creating your own stencil, printing a fragmented stencil, broadening the design of the conventional or ordinary alphabet stencil.

In all of these, and in the Laliberté compositions that follow, the feeling of experimentation as an ingredient vital to the stencilling technique is apparent. Imagination and a simple stencilled letter form can be a wonderful combination, for the solitary letter can be distorted, repeated or overlapped to form a distinctive design, or given an entire personality of its own. The artist is far from bound by the strong and precise form and cut of the stencil; on the contrary, it is at this point where individuality is sparked.

Though the stencil concept or process is traditional, its contemporary technique of application is far from tradition-bound. Laliberté's studies begin with this premise and journey in a number of directions through the use and development of a variety of techniques. Fully conscious of the stencil's potentialities, he creates his own stencil images, prints them, then distorts and distresses them in search of interesting results. He explores with ordinary household objects such as a cookie cutter or a miniature license plate, and through a technique of overlapped impressions we see these familiar forms in a new context. He stencils on top of stencils, monoprints from a stencil, creates intricate stencils with segments of paper doilies, experiments with space and form relationships through stencil repetition. There seem to be no hard or fast rules, only the evolution of processes as the work develops.

The stencil compositions illustrated are a long way from the soft flow of Japanese stencil designs and the precise and organized stencil traditions of the Victorian age. But though different in form, what they have in common is that they are somehow expressive of the time in which they were created. In a highly technical age, the emphasis cannot help but be on originality of technique, and the results that evolve are stimulating, exciting, and extremely free.

The number 23; one half of the number was treated in a solid manner, the other in an opposite technique to produce an interesting overall effect. Projects such as these illustrate the countless ways in which the stencil can be employed to create exciting and stimulating compositions.

Opposite Page

A series of designs created by using only one stencil letter in each composition. In this project the positioning of the letters and the way in which they are moved (reversed, flopped or slightly varied in placement) create new patterns and unusual visual symbols and images.

Above, left. Two numbers have been stencilled with a pen to be overlapped by two other numbers of the same size, traced with a charcoal pencil. The contrast between the free pen line and the shadowy line produced by the charcoal is most effective.

Above, right. Again individual figures are used, but this time the stencil was held above the paper to allow the sunlight to filter through the openings. The shadow of the figures reflected on the paper was traced to produce interesting distortions. By changing the angle at which the light comes through the stencil, a great many distorted variations are possible.

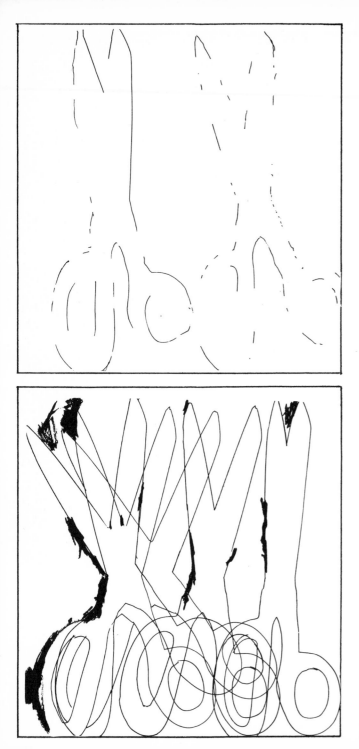
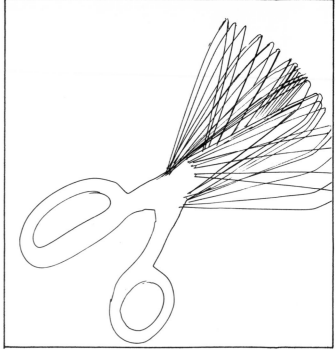

Study of a Pair of Scissors. The tool itself is treated as if it were a stencil. It is outlined with semi-solid and pointillistic lines (above, left); the scissors are fixed at one point, but one blade is allowed to move up and down while its positioning is recorded with a pen outline (above, right); the scissors are moved from left to right, while the blades are opened at a different angle with each change of position and the sequence recorded (below, left). The scissors' outline is again recorded, only this time very distinctly with pen and ink. When the first tracing is complete, the scissors are positioned again so that a minimum of overlapping occurs. This procedure is repeated four times, creating the impression that there are four different pairs of scissors (below, right). Procedures like this have unlimited possibilities and can lead to major paintings and compositions stimulated by ordinary, everyday objects.

A cutout dove is used as a stencil in a number of different positions and various stencil techniques, including negative and positive versions of the bird, overlapping, mirror reversing ("flopping") and off-register printing. This is a good illustration of how one stencilled object can be repeated and used in many directions and moods.

A marble relief of the Greek dramatist Menander (343–291 B.C. ?) holding the mask of the actor who plays the lover, while other masks — those of the father and daughter — rest on the table. Masks played an important role in the dramatic presentations of this early Greek period, engendering a spirit of mystery and intrigue. (Reproduced with the permission of The Art Museum, Princeton.)

MASKS, FACE COVERINGS, AND HEADGEAR

Masks and Headgear
Throughout the Ages

Masks, or the idea of covering or disguising the human face, may be as old as man himself. The origin of the mask is not clear, but evidence of its presence has been found in the artifacts, literature, and lore of practically every society (primitive as well as civilized or sophisticated) known to us today.

The primitives, believing the world to be ruled by spirits or supernatural beings, devised masks and headgear to be worn ceremonially in their attempts to appease or communicate with these forces greater and more powerful than themselves. But the use of masks, carved or fashioned by primitive craftsmen from a wide variety of natural and, in some instances, manufactured materials (including wood, fiber, shell, bone, feathers, stone, hides, ivory, bark, grass, leaves, husks, and other vegeta-

tion and crude metals), was part of everyday life as well. Earlier societies used masks to frighten children as a form of warning or punishment; similarly, masks were worn in battle to terrorize the enemy. Frequently, a primitive family would associate itself with a mythological being, an animal or spirit expressed in the form of a mask, which more or less would come to serve as that group's identifying symbol. Ceremonies devised to appease or enhance this spirit over the years became part of the family's tradition. In addition to having their use in battle, masks were traditionally worn as a disguise (or as a good-luck charm) by tribesmen hunting for food.

Masks were and, to an extent, are an important part of life on many continents. In Africa, masks carved in the likeness of departed

chieftains are still used in elaborate memorial services. North American Indians employed the mask in rain-making ceremonies or as a form of ritual to assure the abundance to their crops. Masks have been used to prevent illness and to cure disease in China, Burma, and Ceylon. Tribes in New Guinea have been known to hold a form of court in which criminals are tried and punished by judges wearing huge masks meant to hide their identity while at the same time serving to enlarge their authority. All of these uses and many, many more, embracing superstition, magic, spiritual and supernatural powers, mythological beings and religious doctrine and dogma, represent a predominant element in the history of a good many societies as expressed through the use of the mask.

209

In a theatrical sense, the mask, frequently supplemented by elaborate headgear, has been prevalent since earliest times. Both the Greeks and Romans in their dramatic presentations used masks and headgear to denote identity or to elaborate on the characteristics of the personality being portrayed. In medieval times, masks and exaggerated headdress were used to dramatize passages from the Bible while hideous masks of dragons and serpents depicted the sins of man. It is believed that many of the Mardi Gras-like festivities carried out today in Europe as well as in parts of the western hemisphere owe their origin to this period. Masked characterizations portrayed a great number of historic, political, and religious personages throughout Europe during the Renaissance. For the most part, these masks — full-faced, half-masks, masks with sharp or beaked noses, masks depicting facial blemishes — originated in Italy, where they were considered an art form.

In the East — Japan, China, Tibet, and Java — the mask assumed significance in drama and ceremony important to both national life and sacred beliefs. The Nō masks of the Japanese, for instance, depict well over one-hundred characters and beings including gods, devils, demons, and a variety of human characterizations. Masked Tibetans resembling ghouls, skeletons, and prehistoric creatures perform a series of devil-dances at different seasons of the year. The Chinese papier-mâché masks perpetuate the religious drama of that people, while in Java, masks made of wood have been known to supplement shadow-play puppet presentations for entertainment and as a form of superstitious expression against natural disaster.

Masks and Headgear in the Professions and Sports

The mask and a variety of headgear are vital to many of today's professions and sports. Consider the quarterback without his helmet and face guard, the beekeeper without the mesh screen surrounding his head, the jet fighter pilot without headgear that protects him from the thrust of the vehicle travelling faster than sound and without the apparatus which gives him both oxygen and communication. In all of these and more, the importance of the mask or the headgear is paramount to the practice of the profession or sport.

Each mask, face covering, helmet, or headgear apparatus has been devised or designed primarily for maximum function within an individual sport or profession. But often the development and use of new materials has produced (many times by accident) esthetic qualities or connotations of mystery and intrigue. The astronaut's one-way face shield protects the wearer from sun and outer space phenomena in terms of light. The images reflected on the one-way glass suggest both anonymity and a 20th century sense of sophistication. The steel worker's asbestos masks shroud the head and shoulders; the varying shapes of the look-out apertures are reminiscent of stories recalling the headgear and apparel of medieval warriors.

In some instances, individuality is a prime consideration in determining the outward appearance of the mask. The clown, for instance, wears his disguise in a pattern, color, and manner that is a particular expression of the comical or whimsical character he portrays. Masks worn by actors and actresses in theatrical presentations in most cases are highly individualized and reflect something of the personality being expressed within the drama being performed. Though masks can be purchased over the counter for participation in most sports, it is interesting to note that many of the professional hockey goaltenders have their plastic masks individually molded so that they conform fully to the shape and contour of the face.

The headgear worn in many professions is practical in a number of instances, but in others it serves merely as a symbol of identification. The cowboy's hat has a function: it protects the wearer from the wind, dust, rain, and the searing sun. But the Playboy bunny girl's "ears" at the top of her head merely serve to identify her role within the environment. Similarly, a nun's headcovering, in addition to symbolizing a sense of humility, accentuates the order to which she belongs, and in most cases hats and headgear worn by army personnel (in addition to indicating that they are all part of the same service) denote rank and/or a particular branch of the organization.

Masks, face coverings, and headgear are important to 20th century life, particularly as we move into both a more specialized and individualistic society, simultaneously. The Afro hair-do, as an example, may not have originated in Africa, but it does serve as an expression of an individual's determination to help achieve certain social and political aspirations for the Black people of North America. And, similarly, though practically all hockey goalies wear masks, the markings that Boston's Gerry Cheevers has carved on his, say in no uncertain way: "I'm not just another hockey player, I am me!"

Opposite Page

The mask is a relatively late arrival to hockey, having become popular with goalies only during the last decade. Gerry Cheevers of the Boston Bruins marks his mask for every time he might have endured a severe injury had he not been wearing it. (Photograph courtesy of the Boston Bruins Hockey Club.)

Page 216

Helmeted football player — Ron Johnson, Giant's first 100-yard rusher. This mask and head covering is strictly functional; it must be strong to withstand collision, while the wire cage serves as a face protector that allows the player to see and breathe. The decorative elements are insignia and numbers for identification purposes. (Photo courtesy The Patent Trader, Mt. Kisco, N.Y.)

Page 217

U.S. Army personnel. The headgear denotes a specific function or branch of the Armed Forces and gives the wearer identity. An historic folklore has evolved about some of the headgear worn. (Photo courtesy of the U.S. Armed Forces.)

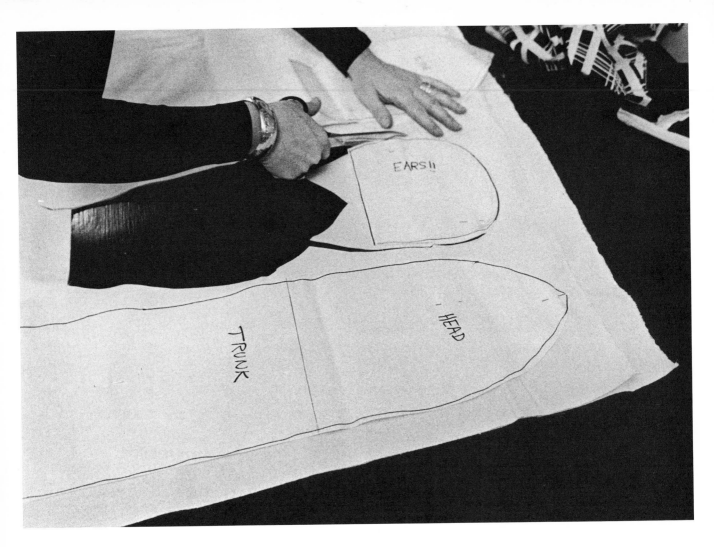

Cutting the Elephant Mask. Straight pins are used to keep the paper pattern pieces flat and stationary against the cloth. The pieces are then cut out following the definition of the pattern. Heavy-weight unbleached muslin material is used for the major part of the mask; decorative elements are devised spontaneously and cut from patterned materials. The pattern consists of the trunk (which includes the front and back of the head), two large ears (which are cut double — for back and front of each ear — out of a patterned cotton voile material), and two side pieces.

Demonstration: The Elephant Mask

This chapter features a demonstration in mask-making by Sas Colby, who makes cloth come to life in a number of striking and colorful forms including clothing and costuming, dolls and masks. She is a craftsman particularly conscious of color, pattern, weight, and texture of materials, and she succeeds in giving these elements an impressive and integral role in her finished creations.

Sas Colby works in the excitement of celebration and joy, qualities which are inherent in the masks and costuming she produces. Whether it is a mask or a cape which she has designed, the emphasis is on the very richness of the satin or velvet she has used, and the sensual feeling which seems to radiate in the act of wearing.

"It enlarges you," she feels. "It allows you to act the grand entrance, the self-confident swagger that is, of course, the real you. You have visions of Byzantine richness, Renaissance glory, King Arthur's Court. You could be there; or you could be here now. Life is to celebrate!"

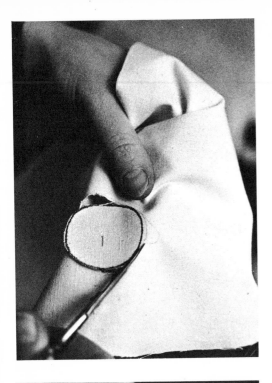

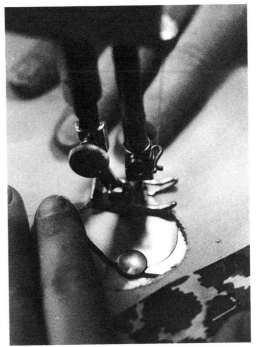

Above, left. Cutting the eyes out of the material. *Above, right.* The holes for the eyes are outlined with zig-zag machine stitching to prevent the material from shredding or un-ravelling. This is done before cording is stitched onto eye. *Below, left.* Trimming a piece of eyelet material which will add a decorative element to the nose. *Below, right.* Putting the decorative nose pieces into place. These are straight-pinned into position before sewing. A darker thread is used to sew them permanently into place, to accentuate the in-dividual features. If necessary, zig-zag sewing is repeated, one sequence over the other, depen-ding on how pronounced the line of the decorative element is to be.

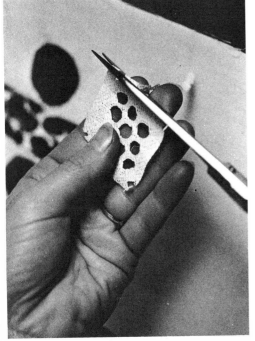

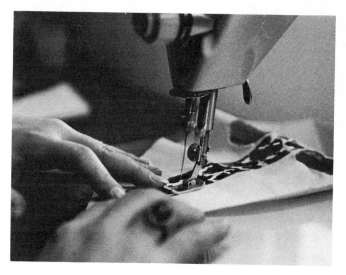

Above, left. Cutting selected elements from a patterned piece of cloth to provide decorative detail to the mask. *Above, right.* Fitting the elements into place. This is a spontaneous procedure; frequently the precise nature of a material will suggest a decorative motif for the mask. Once started, the mask just seems to grow! Compare the mask at this stage with completed illustration, top of page 53. *Below, left.* Close-up of patterned material. *Below, right.* Zig-zag stitching the decorative element into permanent place. Zig-zag stitching is repeated several times to emphasize and define the line of the decorative detail.

Above, left. Decoratively covered cording is sewn around the perimeters of the eyes and the ears to give these features definition and body. The bare cording is covered with patterned cloth which has been cut on the bias for flexibility. Here, the cloth is being hand-sewn around the cording.

Above, right. Close-up of patterned cloth being hand-sewn to cover bare cording.

Below, left. Fitting the covered cording around the eye circumference. Note: the cording is stitched onto the face of the mask from the reverse (or underside) so that the stitches which hold it onto the mask will not show or be obvious.

Below, right. Front view of the completed, highly decorative Elephant Mask.

Opposite Page

A mask made of cut corrugated cardboard pieces by Norman Laliberté.

222

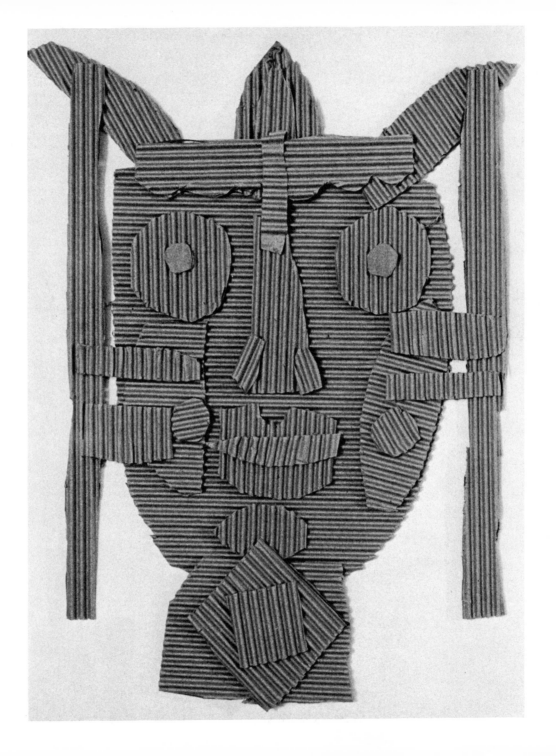

Electro Projectile Light Masks created by Bob and Edrea Hanson of New York City. The face becomes the screen for constantly changing projected images. Each projection creates both a mask and a mood of mystical and haunting quality. There are many exciting aspects to mask-making through this electronic — projection medium. For instance, an old man's face can be projected onto the countenance of a youth; any number of such intriguing mask potentialities are possible. Another attribute is the speed at which a mask can change. The mind hardly has had time to adjust to and accept one mask image, when suddenly it is confronted with another and still another! (Reproduction courtesy of Bob and Edrea Hanson.)